Keto Diabetic Cookbook and Meal Plan

Keto Diabetic Cookbook

AND MEAL PLAN

4-WEEK KETO DIET MEAL PLAN FOR TYPE 2 DIABETES

JENNIFER ALLEN

HEATHER AYALA, MS, RD, CKNS

Photography by Darren Muir

ROCKRIDGE
PRESS

First Rockridge Press trade paperback edition July 2022

Rockridge Press and the Rockridge Press logo are trademarks or registered trademarks of Callisto Media Inc. and/or its affiliates in the United States and other countries and may not be used without written permission.

For general information on our other products and services, please contact our Customer Care Department within the United States at (866) 744-2665, or outside the United States at (510) 253-0500.

Paperback ISBN: 978-1-63878-351-0
eBook ISBN: 978-1-63878-576-7

Manufactured in the United States of America

Interior and Cover Designer: Patricia Fabricant
Art Producer: Samantha Ulban
Editor: Anna Pulley
Production Manager: Lanore Coloprisco

Photography © 2022 Darren Muir. Food styling by Yolanda Muir.

10 9 8 7 6 5 4 3 2 1 0

Jennifer Allen: To my family, who have supported me dealing with type 2 diabetes and who give the best feedback when I'm creating new recipes.

Heather Ayala: To my husband, for supporting me. To my kiddos, for eating whatever is served and not complaining too much.

CONTENTS

INTRODUCTION

I stumbled onto keto completely by accident. I was teaching a seminar on basic nutrition principles in 2016, and an attendee asked me what I thought about the keto diet. As any registered dietitian working on her master of science degree in nutritional science would have said back then, I advised her that "restrictive diets that eliminate whole food groups are not recommended because they are impractical and unsustainable." Oh boy. Later that week, I had an epiphany. I realized that I knew next to nothing about the keto diet and should probably keep my professional opinions to myself until I was better informed. I started researching that day and didn't come up for breath until I had read every piece of research, watched every educational video, and did a deep dive putting what I'd learned into practice for myself. Four years later, I have my board certification in ketogenic nutrition from the American Nutrition Association and am always happy to promote this way of eating to clients when appropriate.

My family's medical history is full of diabetes, neurodegenerative disorders, cardiac events, mental illness, and cancer. I have watched so many loved ones struggle with the standard advice on how to manage their chronic illnesses, but none so much as diabetes. The standard of care for chronic disease does not involve much nutrition education, if any, and leads many to believe that they have a hopeless, progressive condition with an unavoidably bleak future. Pretty sad when you learn that some simple dietary changes can normalize your blood sugar and potentially help you get off some of your medications! Research has shown that the ketogenic diet is a safe and effective tool to help those with type 2 diabetes manage their blood sugar and improve their long-term outcomes.

Part of the reason medical professionals might be more willing to hand out a prescription than promote a lifestyle change such as diet modification is this: Changing your eating habits can be challenging. Well, there is help for you in this book. My four-week meal plan can help make the change to a keto lifestyle easier by taking the planning off your hands, all while satisfying your taste buds and training your culinary skills in the way of keto cooking. And when you've worked through the meal plan, you can start again and go another four weeks, or you can mix and match the recipes to make a new four-week plan for yourself or use those new culinary skills to come up with your own plan.

We designed this book to accompany you on your journey, and we recommend you start at the beginning and take it one step at a time. There's no rush. Knowledge is power, which is why we recommend that you read through the first chapter and make sure you understand the principles of diabetes and the ketogenic diet before you dive into the recipes and meal plan. You can always come back to chapter 1 for a refresher or if you need some help explaining your new way of life to someone who doesn't understand keto.

STRAWBERRY SMOOTHIE, PAGE 44

CHAPTER ONE

Diabetes and the Keto Diet

EVERY NONFIBER CARBOHYDRATE YOU EAT becomes sugar in your blood. Diabetes makes it difficult for your body to use that sugar for energy and keep the amount in your blood within a healthy range. A ketogenic diet helps by keeping your carbohydrate intake low, thus keeping high amounts of sugar out of your blood in the first place.

Since the hallmark of diabetes is high blood sugar and the ketogenic diet reduces blood sugar by restricting the intake of carbohydrates, it's a match made in metabolic heaven. In this chapter, you'll learn more about diabetes, the ketogenic diet, and how this way of eating is just what the doctor (probably should have) ordered.

UNDERSTANDING TYPE 2 DIABETES

Diabetes is a condition that, left unmanaged, leads to chronic high levels of sugar in the blood. Your blood should always have some sugar in it, with the normal fasting range being 70 to 110 mg/dl. This range equates to about a teaspoon of sugar (4 grams) in your entire blood volume at any one time. This amount is quite remarkable, considering that every nonfiber carbohydrate we consume gets converted into sugar, in addition to all the natural and added sugar we eat. So where does all that sugar go if it's not hanging out in your blood?

Insulin

When you consume something that raises your blood sugar, a hormone called insulin is produced and released by the pancreas and gets to work. Insulin unlocks the sugar gates of just about every cell in your body to allow sugar in to be used as energy. It also closes the gates of your energy storage in your fat cells and liver to prevent more energy from entering the blood while it is dealing with the energy you just consumed. Before you know it, all that sugar energy in your blood is packed into your cells, and you are energized and ready for action. At least, that's what is supposed to happen.

Insulin Resistance

When you have type 2 diabetes, also known as insulin-resistant diabetes, your cells are resistant to the action of insulin, and you need more and more of it to unlock the sugar gates. Your cells have become tired of sugar and start ignoring insulin's knock at the door, so the pancreas sends more insulin to the doors to "force" them open. At some point, your pancreas becomes unable to keep up with the demand for insulin, and more and more of the sugar stays in your blood. You may have symptoms of fatigue, frequent urination (to expel the excess sugar), frequent thirst (to dilute the excess sugar and help expel it), unexplained weight loss, or blurred vision.

MANAGING YOUR BLOOD SUGAR

Some of the sugar in your blood attaches to hemoglobin in your red blood cells and stays attached for the life cycle of each cell—about three months. High blood sugar means more sugar attached to red blood cells; lower blood sugar means less is attached. Because of this phenomenon, a common lab test to detect diabetes is the Hemoglobin A1C (abbreviated as A1C or HgbA1C).

According to the American Diabetes Association, an A1C of less than 5.7% is normal, A1Cs in the range of 5.7–6.5% indicate prediabetes (and average blood sugar of 120–140 mg/dl), and A1Cs above 6.5% indicate diabetes. A1Cs above 9% are considered severe and indicate an average blood sugar of 212 mg/dl, although I have seen individuals with A1Cs as high as 17% in clinical practice. This is the equivalent of having an *average* blood sugar of 600 mg/dl. If you are diabetic, reducing your A1C to less than 7% is a common target of most interventions.

LIVING WITH TYPE 2 DIABETES

A diabetes diagnosis can be scary, but it is definitely not a death sentence. Instead, consider it as inspiration for a new beginning. You can do many things to manage and improve this condition. Some research shows that it can even be put into remission, with a decreased need for medication, if blood sugar is brought into a normal range and maintained through lifestyle changes. Let's take a look at some of the most impactful things you can do to take care of your health and improve your blood sugar.

Exercise

Exercise is an important part of any healthy lifestyle—this much we know. But do you know how vital it is for those with diabetes? When you exercise in any capacity, your muscle cells recognize the need for energy and become more sensitive to the effects of insulin, eagerly opening up those sugar gates and pulling more sugar out of the blood. Your muscle cells, when actively working, can even pull sugar directly without relying on insulin. And the exercise doesn't have to be very intense, either. Simply going for a 30-minute walk is worth something. If you can increase intensity and duration, even better. Try getting some steps in after every meal or keep weights near your bed and do some light lifting when you wake up.

Another often-overlooked benefit of exercise is known as afterburn. Up to 24 hours after you work out, depending on the length of time and the intensity, your body may still pull sugar out of your blood to restock your muscles' supply. The more intense the workout, or the longer you are active, the more sugar you use during the activity and in the 24 hours afterward. If you are on medication that lowers blood sugar, you should talk with your doctor before starting a new exercise routine, since the afterburn effect could potentially cause low blood sugar (hypoglycemia).

Medication

Many individuals who walk out of their doctor's office with a type 2 diabetes diagnosis also leave with a prescription to help them manage their blood sugar levels (likely without much information on what to eat, arguably the most important thing to know). There are several types of medications prescribed for diabetes management, and some of the most common are in the following table.

TYPE OF MEDICATION	GENERIC NAME	ACTION
Alpha-glucosidase inhibitor	Acarbose Miglitol	Blocks the breakdown and absorption of starches and sugars
Biguanide	Metformin	Decreases sugar production in the liver and sugar absorption in the intestines, and increases insulin sensitivity
Dipeptidyl peptidase-4 (DPP-4) inhibitor	Sitagliptin phosphate	Increases insulin production by the pancreas
Glucagon-like peptide-1 (GLP-1) receptor agonist	Liraglutide	Increases insulin production and utilization, slows stomach emptying
Insulin	Glargine Aspart Lispro Detemir	Helps cells take up glucose from the blood

TYPE OF MEDICATION	GENERIC NAME	ACTION
Sodium-glucose transporter 2 (SGLT2) inhibitor	Canagliflozin	Increases the output of glucose through the kidneys in the urine
Sulfonylurea	Glipizide Glimepiride Glyburide	Increases insulin production by the pancreas
Thiazolidinedione	Pioglitazone hydrochloride	Decreases sugar production by the liver, increases fat-cell sensitivity to insulin

This table does not list every medication your doctor may prescribe to help you manage your diabetes. If you have any questions about the actions of your medications or their side effects, make sure to talk with your doctor or pharmacist.

A note of caution for those who are on blood-sugar-lowering medications: Work closely with your prescribing physician when embarking on a keto journey, because severely low blood sugar may occur. Chronic high blood sugar can cause many health complications in the long run, but one critically low blood sugar reading can be fatal.

Diet

You are not alone if you were not educated on an appropriate diet to manage your blood sugar when you received your diabetes diagnosis. A study conducted in 2018 in the UK found that most individuals with diabetes surveyed received either no or insufficient diet education with their A1C results, leaving them feeling "tested but not educated." Although what you eat directly impacts your blood sugar, many doctors are not well trained in nutrition and often fail to refer their patients to someone who can help in that department (i.e., a registered dietitian). That situation might be what brought you to this book. Continue reading to learn everything you need to know about how different foods affect your blood sugar, what you can eat to stay healthy and reduce your A1C, and guidance on how to adapt to and maintain beneficial eating habits.

TYPE 2 DIABETES AND YOUR HEALTH

Chronically elevated blood sugar produces a host of poor health outcomes. There is no body system that is not negatively affected if your blood sugar remains out of control for too long. Here is a list of some of the most common consequences that can occur:

Cancer: There is no direct evidence linking high blood sugar to the cause of cancer, but many studies, starting with researchers in the 1920s, have shown that many types of cancer feed on sugar, making uncontrolled diabetes a risk factor for poor cancer outcomes.

Heart disease: Inflammation created by chronic high blood sugar can impact your heart and circulatory system, causing cholesterol levels to increase, which is likely why individuals with poorly managed diabetes are twice as likely than someone without diabetes to suffer from a heart attack or stroke, according to the Centers for Disease Control.

Lost eyesight: The vessels at the back of the eye are very small and sensitive, and high blood sugar damages them easily, leading to blurry vision, night blindness, and potentially even complete blindness.

Nerve damage: The effects of this are wide-ranging, from decreased gut motility resulting in poor digestion, to pain and tingling in the arms and legs, to dementia.

Poor wound healing: This is perhaps one of the more dangerous side effects of chronically elevated blood sugar. The high sugar impairs the ability of wounds to close up and also increases the likelihood of infection, which can cause further damage and spread to other parts of the body. If severe enough, this could even cause the need for amputations.

All these poor outcomes can be mitigated or even outright avoided if you can maintain blood sugar levels within normal limits using the lifestyle changes and medication (if needed) previously mentioned.

▍NUTRITION AND DIABETES

Nothing impacts your blood sugar more than what you choose to eat. If you are going to leverage nutrition to help you fight against diabetes, you need to know which foods will help you in that journey and which will set you back.

Before you start thinking of foods as "good" or "bad," remember that all foods can fit in a healthy diet. Yes, all foods. And this dietitian is giving you full permission to eat whatever you want. Now, that comes with some caveats, of course. If you pay attention to how your food choices impact your goals and your health, I hope you will want to choose foods that nourish you and support your health most of the time. You may *crave* that high-sugar blended coffee beverage topped with whipped cream and syrup, but once you know how it will impact your blood sugar and your health, will you *really* want it? Cravings are not hunger, and you've got big plans for your life, so remember that when such temptations confront you. And if you still decide you want that treat, go for it! No guilt or shame. Go into it with the full knowledge of what it is and what impact it will have, know that it is worth it to you at that moment, and enjoy. As an alternative, consider that there is probably a delicious keto version of whatever you are craving (check out the recipes in chapter 9), which will allow you to indulge that craving while still sticking to your goals.

▍Carbohydrates

Our diets have macronutrients (the big ones that give us energy and structure: carbohydrates, protein, and fat) and micronutrients (the little ones that give us function: vitamins and minerals). We will focus primarily on macronutrients, but specific micronutrients are important in a ketogenic diet, and we will talk about those as well.

Of all the nutrients we will be talking about, carbohydrates are the ones you need to become the most familiar with because they have the most impact on your blood sugar levels. Your intake of carbohydrates (or lack thereof) is the leading driver of the ketogenic diet and the main determinant of whether you will be in ketosis. Carbohydrates come in three main classifications: fiber, starch, and sugar.

Fiber is a type of carbohydrate that you do not digest and absorb, so it doesn't raise your blood sugar. It does feed your gut microbiome, which is an important part of health. Fiber from whole-food sources is a big part of a healthy ketogenic diet. Starch and sugar (natural or added) are the two main carbohydrates that raise your blood sugar, so they are very limited in the keto diet.

Every plant that you consume contains carbohydrates. Some of those carbohydrates are fiber, some are starch, and some are sugar. Dairy products also have some carbohydrates in them in the form of lactose, which is a type of sugar. Other animal products, other than honey, contain only minute amounts of carbohydrates, which is why most ketogenic ways of eating include them as a significant portion of most meals.

A fun fact for you: There is no such thing as an "essential" carbohydrate. Your red blood cells are the only cells in your body that can survive on nothing but glucose, but your body can make every bit of carbohydrate it needs to function through a process called gluconeogenesis, which takes place in your liver. This is not true for fat and protein, though.

Protein

Protein is an essential nutrient, meaning that you cannot make all you need. You have to get it from outside sources, which is food. Protein is made up of amino acids, and your body can make about half of the amino acids you need, but you have to bring in the other half through your diet. Animal proteins (meat, fish, eggs, dairy, poultry) provide adequate amounts of all essential amino acids. Plant proteins (beans, nuts, seeds, grains) provide only some essential amino acids or don't provide them in large enough quantities. This means that you need to eat a large variety and amount of plant-based proteins to ensure that you meet your needs. Following a ketogenic diet while primarily getting your protein from plants would be very challenging.

Fat

Long demonized as the cause of heart disease, fat is having a comeback as old research is re-examined and new research is conducted. Far from being something to avoid, fat benefits our bodies in many ways, and our brains and nervous systems are primarily composed of fat. Not to mention that a layer of fat (the lipid bilayer cell membrane) covers every cell in your body.

You consume several types of fats, and their names relate to the amounts of hydrogen they contain. Saturated fats are full of (a.k.a. saturated with) hydrogen. Because of their chemical structure, these fats appear solid at room temperature. Foods rich in saturated fat include butter, lard, and coconut oil. Your body can

RETHINKING SATURATED FATS

Diabetes is a disease of poor carbohydrate utilization in the body, and it surprises me how many doctors prioritize advising their new diabetic patients to reduce their saturated fat intake. The problem with this advice is it is outdated and controversial. In a state of ketosis, with blood sugar well controlled in a normal range, your body readily uses fat, especially saturated fat, for energy. Limiting saturated fat on a ketogenic diet, even for the treatment of diabetes, may not be easy or even necessary. The scientific research is still divided on this, though, and it may be some time before the medical community can come to a consensus. If you or your doctor are concerned, a great recommendation is to aim for a Mediterranean-style diet with your protein and fat choices. This means limiting your intake of red and processed meats, enjoying regular consumption of fish, and using more olive oil than butter. The Mediterranean diet is one of the most well-studied diets in the world and is consistently ranked as one of the healthiest as well. Some of the reasons may be its high level of monounsaturated and omega-3 fatty acids and its low amounts of saturated fat.

make all the saturated fat that it needs and readily uses the saturated fat you eat to store energy as triglycerides in your fat cells. These triglycerides can then be used for energy to power your day, especially in a fasted or ketogenic state, and to make the glucose your red blood cells need in the absence of carbohydrates.

Unsaturated fats have one or more spots where there could be hydrogen but there is not. This means they are not saturated with hydrogen (a.k.a. unsaturated). Foods rich in this type of fat are liquid at room temperature, such as olive oil and canola oil. Monounsaturated fats have one available spot for hydrogen, and polyunsaturated fats have two or more. The only essential fats we need to consume are the polyunsaturated fats DHA and EPA. The best sources of these fats are seafood that lives in cold waters, with some of the richest sources being caviar, sardines, and salmon.

The other type of fat to be aware of is trans fat, a.k.a. partially hydrogenated oil. This fat is unsaturated fat that has been artificially saturated with hydrogen to improve its shelf life and mouthfeel. These have proven to be detrimental to cardiac health and have largely disappeared from our food supply, but they can occasionally appear in some highly processed foods. Check ingredient labels to make sure you are avoiding sources of trans fat.

Electrolytes

If you eat a balanced diet with plenty of protein and non-starchy fruits and vegetables, you will easily meet your daily recommended micronutrient (vitamin and mineral) needs. On a ketogenic diet, though, some minerals are conditionally essential, meaning you need more of them due to being in a special metabolic state. These are calcium, potassium, magnesium, and sodium. The reason you need more of these particular minerals, which are also called electrolytes (because they help your nervous system conduct electricity), is complex. Essentially, being in a ketogenic state causes your kidneys to eliminate more of these minerals, along with more water. The best way to manage this increased need is to make special effort to consume foods high in these nutrients and to liberally salt your foods. Some keto-friendly foods rich in electrolytes are avocados, leafy greens, cheese, nuts, seeds, and pickles. You can also consume an electrolyte-containing beverage, but make sure it is not sweetened with sugar and that it contains each of the electrolytes mentioned.

Water

As mentioned previously, in a ketogenic state the kidneys are prone to releasing more water, which makes it especially important that you drink plenty every day to stay hydrated. A good rule of thumb is to drink about half your body weight in ounces. For example, if you weigh 150 pounds, a good starting point is to consume about 75 ounces of water. You can drink more or less, using the color of your urine as a guide. Optimal hydration produces very light-yellow urine. If it is too dark, you are not drinking enough. If it has no color, you may be overly hydrated and need to cut back a bit.

THE KETO DIET VERSUS THE DIABETIC DIET

The ketogenic diet essentially replaces the carbohydrate-rich foods of the Diabetic Plate with foods rich in fat and fiber. By eliminating foods that put large amounts of sugar into the blood, the body is forced to work through its stores of sugar in the liver and muscle. Those stores are replenished by breaking down fat, either from the diet or from fat cells, and the body switches to using fat and fat-derived

THE DIABETIC PLATE DIET

The American Diabetes Association designed the Diabetic Plate as general guidance for those needing a visual example of building a healthy diet to manage their blood sugar. It recommends that one-quarter of your plate be carbohydrate-rich foods such as fruits and starchy vegetables, one-quarter of your plate be protein, and half of your plate be non-starchy vegetables. An ideal plate might look like a baked potato, grilled chicken, and a salad, which sounds balanced. This method, though, equates high-sugar fruits like bananas with low-sugar fruits like berries. The sugar load of plates with those different kinds of fruits would be widely different and should not be considered equivalent. Fats are largely ignored on the plate, and someone following this method may not consume an adequate amount for health and satiety and could easily consume too many carbohydrates for optimal blood sugar control.

In contrast to the Diabetic Plate, a keto diabetic plate might look like this: one-quarter animal-based protein, one-quarter healthy fat, and one-half non-starchy vegetables. Low-carb fruits may be eaten, but only in small amounts, which is why they aren't included on the main plate. Near the end of this chapter, I'll provide a breakdown of foods that fit nicely onto a keto plate and some foods that you will need to restrict or avoid to achieve and maintain ketosis.

molecules known as ketones for energy. This shifts the body into a novel metabolic state: ketosis.

If you can control your blood sugar by following the Diabetic Plate method, maybe that feels like a less extreme protocol to follow. It is a bit looser and may feel a little bit closer to your typical diet. However, the lack of clear guidance on specific foods, such as dairy and added sugars, could potentially be a hurdle that prevents you from reaching your blood sugar goals.

A study published in 2017 in the *Journal of Medical Internet Research* compared the plate method with the ketogenic diet as far as outcomes for individuals with type 2 diabetes. They found the ketogenic diet significantly more effective for weight loss and reduction in A1C to the normal range. This is something to consider when you are making your choice about which protocol to follow. In the end, though, the diet you will stick to is the one that works. We hope you will give the ketogenic diet a try, and that you will use the information and recipes in this book to make it easier and a more sustainable lifestyle change for yourself.

A KETO PRIMER FOR TYPE 2 DIABETES

At this point you have a good understanding of what diabetes is and how and why the ketogenic diet is an effective treatment tool to use in blood sugar management. There are some other principles that are important to know before you embark on this journey, including what exactly to eat, how to know whether you are in ketosis, and what you need to prepare for this journey.

Carbs in Focus

An important principle to know in the ketogenic diet is how to count carbohydrates. Again, the main determinant of whether you will achieve a state of ketosis is how low your intake is of foods that raise your blood sugar. Remember what was mentioned before about carbohydrates not being an "essential" nutrient? It's true. The only cells in your body that can only use glucose for energy are your red blood cells, and your liver truly can make as much as they need. This makes it theoretically possible for you to consume absolutely zero carbohydrates and still function normally. This is a huge premise behind the rise in popularity of carnivore diets, which rely completely on animal products such as meat, organs, and eggs. The ketogenic diet is not quite that extreme, though, and only calls for you to drop your carbohydrate intake low enough for your body to enter a state of ketosis. This amount is different for everyone, but a baseline recommendation is about 20 grams of net carbs per day.

Remember that reducing your carbohydrate intake on medications that lower blood sugar can be dangerous. Please plan to work closely with your physician, especially as you transition from your current diet into a state of ketosis, as de-prescription may be necessary to prevent hypoglycemia.

Testing for Ketones

You can look for some symptoms to tell that you are in ketosis (such as mildly fruity smelling breath, rapid weight loss, especially in the first week or two, increased focus and mental clarity, and decreased appetite), but often these are subjective and not reliable. Two more reliable methods are testing your urine or blood. Testing

IS KETO RIGHT FOR YOU?

The ketogenic diet can be one of the most important tools that someone with diabetes can use to manage their blood sugar, but it is not for everyone. Let's look at some situations that require greater caution.

Cardiovascular disease: Again, due to the wide variety and degree of cardiovascular issues, it is difficult to make a safe, broad recommendation for a ketogenic diet to this population. Changes in electrolytes and the types and amounts of fats in the blood, especially during the adaptation phase, could spell danger if not monitored closely.

Eating disorders: Following any strict dietary pattern can be triggering for those who have suffered or who are currently suffering from an eating disorder.

Pregnancy: Ketones are naturally higher and insulin resistance is present to some degree in pregnancy. It is believed that these two processes occur to ensure adequate energy is always available in the mother's bloodstream to cross the placenta to the developing baby. Despite this information, though, there is not enough research to support the safety of following a strict ketogenic diet while pregnant, even if the pregnant person was following a ketogenic diet before.

Renal disease: Depending on the particular type and degree of renal disease, protein requirements and waste filtration by the kidneys are highly variable, making it difficult to ensure safety on a ketogenic diet with broad recommendations.

Type 1 diabetes: Due to an insufficient or nonexistent ability to produce their own insulin, individuals with this condition rely on dosing insulin from external sources, and the risk of low blood sugar is much higher. A transition to a low-carb or ketogenic diet without proper medical oversight can result in critically low blood sugar very quickly.

If you have any of these conditions or any other medical concerns, do not embark on this or any other major dietary change before consulting with a medical professional.

COUNTING CARBS

There are two schools of thought for counting carbs—the total carb counters and the net carb counters. The camp of net carbs recommends subtracting certain carbohydrates that have little to no effect on blood sugar, such as fiber and sugar alcohols. For example, a medium avocado has about 17 grams of total carbohydrates, but 13 of those are fiber. Subtracting the fiber, you would end up with 4 grams of net carbs. The problem is that some fibers have a bigger impact on blood sugar than others, and some people are more sensitive to their effect. The camp of total carbs recommends that you restrict your TOTAL carbohydrate intake (including fiber and sugar alcohols), due to their potentially unpredictable effect on blood sugar. The problem with this is that the diet can become too restrictive, and it may be difficult to consume a wide enough variety of healthy foods without going over your carb limit. If you set your carb limit at 20 grams of total carbs, that avocado would have you almost at your limit, possibly making it difficult to eat balanced meals the rest of the day.

Many people can achieve ketosis using net carbs, especially if they focus on real food instead of processed foods like keto bars and sugar-free treats. If you are having difficulty achieving ketosis using net carbs, either reduce the number of net carbs you consume or try switching to counting total carbs to see if that helps.

ketones in your urine is inexpensive and requires you to keep a container of test strips on hand. You can find them typically in the diabetes supply area of your local pharmacy or online, and they usually cost somewhere around $10 to $15 for 50 to 100 strips. Follow the instructions on the package and aim for low to moderate ketone levels. If your ketones are in the high range, following up with your physician is recommended, especially if you check your blood sugar and it is also high, as this could be evidence of ketoacidosis (see sidebar on page 15). You can also purchase a device that checks your blood ketones, similar to what you use to check your blood sugar, but knowing your ketone level to that degree of specificity is unnecessary for managing type 2 diabetes. If you are interested in using this testing method, several devices are available that can check both ketones and glucose. Expect to spend around 50 cents to $1 per ketone testing strip, though, which can get expensive.

KETOSIS, KETO FLU, AND KETOACIDOSIS

When adapting to ketosis, some metabolic shifts occur. One of the most significant is the release of carbohydrate stores from the liver and muscles. With the utilization of these stores, water is released and expelled by the kidneys. Along with that water comes electrolytes. This rapid drop in availability of sugar, water, and electrolytes may be responsible for the nausea, headache, and shakiness that accompany this transition and are collectively known as "the keto flu." Suffering from these symptoms can largely be mitigated by doing what I call a "low-carb lead-in" before going full keto. Before diving into keto, give yourself a week to eliminate all added sugars and all grains, while enjoying all of the natural sugar in fruit and all of the starchy vegetables you would like. This will slow down the process of emptying your liver and muscles of their carbohydrate stores, thus slowing down the rate of water and electrolyte loss and making for a much smoother transition into full keto.

Ketoacidosis is a critical situation where blood glucose and blood ketones are both high. This happens when carbohydrates are consumed but insulin is insufficient to deal with the load. The cells are not getting the signal that sugar is available, so the body starts to break down fat for energy and shift into a state of ketosis, but now the blood is filled with both sugar and ketones, causing glucose levels often above 300 mg/dl and concurrent moderate or high levels of ketones. Symptoms of this can include insatiable thirst, frequent urination, rapid breathing, nausea and vomiting, and severe tiredness. Keto flu and ketoacidosis symptoms do have some overlap, but testing your blood sugar with a glucometer and your ketones with a urine or blood test can help you determine the cause of your symptoms. If you cannot test, are at high risk of ketoacidosis, or are having significant symptoms, calling your doctor is advised.

YOUR DIABETIC KETO KITCHEN

Changing your diet is challenging, but preparation is half the battle. One strategy I like to use is a pantry cleanse. This involves opening up those cupboards, looking at what is inside, and donating or tossing anything that doesn't fit with your new way of eating. You can use the carb counting strategies you have learned in this book to read food labels, and the food lists on page 16 are another handy guide to

	FOODS TO CHOOSE	FOODS TO MODERATE	FOODS TO AVOID
PROTEINS	Beef, Chorizo, Eggs, Fish, Organ meats, Pork, Poultry, Sausage, Shellfish	Milk, Plain yogurt, Processed meats	
VEGETABLES	Asparagus, Cruciferous vegetables (broccoli, cauliflower, Brussels sprouts, cabbage), Cucumbers, Green beans, Leafy greens, Mushrooms, Raw tomatoes, Sprouts, Zucchini	Artichokes, Baby corn, Bell peppers, Carrots, Cooked tomatoes, Onions, Squash	Legumes, Peas, Potatoes
FRUITS	Avocado, Berries (blueberries, strawberries, blackberries, etc.), Coconut, Lemons, Limes		Apples, Bananas, Fruit juice, Grapes, Kiwi, Oranges, Other melons, Peaches, Pears, Pineapple, Plums, Watermelon
ADDED FATS	Avocado oil, Butter, Cheese, Chia seeds, Coconut oil, Full-fat coconut milk, Ghee, Macadamia nuts, Mayonnaise, Olive oil, Pecans, Pork rinds, Sour cream	Almonds, Canola oil, Cream cheese, Heavy cream, Nut butters, Peanuts, Pistachios, Sunflower seeds	Cashews, Corn oil, Margarine
GRAINS			Corn, Oats, Rice, Wheat

help you know what to keep and what to toss. Don't forget to check the fridge and freezer as well. Sauces and frozen convenience items are large contributors of carbohydrates, especially sugar. Once all the high-carb items are removed from your kitchen, you will be ready to use the shopping list on page 24 to restock it with everything you will need to follow the four-week meal plan.

This list is not exhaustive. If you don't know whether a food is appropriate for your ketogenic diet, there are food tracking apps that can help and many reputable websites you can also use as resources.

KEEPING IT SWEET

What can ketogenic dieters do to include some sweetness in their diet without adding sugar? The most common sweeteners used in ketogenic cooking and baking are sugar alcohols (with erythritol being the most common), stevia, monk fruit, and allulose, which are all considered natural sweeteners. You can also use artificial sweeteners, as they do not raise blood sugar.

Sugar alcohols are a type of carbohydrate that is poorly used for energy, if at all. "Alcohol" in the name is a chemistry term and has to do with a molecule that contains a hydroxide group; it's not the kind of alcohol that gets you drunk. Individuals counting their net carbs (rather than their total carbs) would subtract these from their count. The most common sugar alcohols in keto products are maltitol, xylitol, and erythritol. Since these are largely unused by the body, they tend to stick around in the gut, feeding the microbiome and potentially causing GI distress. When switching to using these types of sweeteners, it is recommended that you start at a low dose and increase as tolerated.

Cooking with these alternative sweeteners can be different from cooking with regular sugar. Use the recipes in this book to help you learn this new skill.

ABOUT THE FOUR-WEEK MEAL PLANS AND RECIPES

It's time to put your knowledge into action and enjoy a wide variety of keto-friendly recipes. There are 80 recipes in this book, covering breakfast to dinner, beverages, and everything in between, as well as prep, variation, and storage tips to make this transition as effortless and tasty as possible. The four weeks of meal plans are designed to help you ease into the keto diet for type 2 diabetes without having to worry about whether you are meeting your nutrient targets each day. By the end of the four weeks, we hope you will have had time to problem-solve and determine what is working for you and what you need to modify for the next four weeks of your journey and beyond. You will have a handle on and improve your skills and intuition when it comes to keto cooking and have a chance to monitor your personal satiety levels, weight changes, and necessary carb level to achieve ketosis.

We've also included the following labels on each recipe for your convenience and dietary or allergy considerations: Vegetarian, Dairy-Free, Gluten-Free, Nut-Free, and Soy-Free.

You have done a lot to prepare yourself for this journey and are probably ready to dive right in. Despite your readiness and eagerness, though, I do recommend you take a week to do that low-carb lead-in, where you cut out all added sugars and grains so you don't crash into keto and suffer from the keto flu. I know it can be challenging to take it slow, but I promise you won't regret it. You can use this lead-in time to gather your needed supplies, clean out your kitchen, and restock with all your new keto-friendly food items.

Don't forget to come back to this chapter if you need a refresher on how and why the ketogenic diet is so effective for managing type 2 diabetes, or if you need talking points to promote and explain this way of eating to others who are skeptical or who may benefit from this information as well.

Keep your focus on what inspired you to make this lifestyle change, and enjoy the journey.

MEATBALL AND ZUCCHINI NOODLE SOUP, PAGE 64

CHAPTER TWO

Four-Week Keto Diabetic Meal Plan

WELCOME TO THE MEAL PLAN portion of this book. Hopefully, by now, you've had a chance to read through the introductory chapter and have taken our advice to ease into starting your keto meal plan. In the following section you'll find meals mapped out for you so you never have to wonder what to eat for breakfast, lunch, or dinner. Optional snacks and desserts are also included, in case you need a bit more to eat in a day. And, to make things even easier, there are weekly shopping lists and lots of tips to help you set up for success.

Are you ready? Let's get started.

▍WEEK 1

▍About the Plan

You might be wondering why you should follow a meal plan. Meal plans take the guesswork out of what to eat and help you get accustomed to keto-friendly ingredients. Have you ever stared into the fridge, wondering what to make for dinner? This meal plan is your answer to that.

Meal plans also help you stay on target. When you know what you're eating for your next meal, you'll be less inclined to give in to temptation and eat things you don't want to eat.

This meal plan is designed so you consume less than 20 net carbs per day, but the menu isn't set in stone. There are plenty of delicious recipes in the book, and you can mix and match or swap out recipes from the meal plan and replace them with a recipe that catches your eye. Just recalculate the macros or net carbs to ensure you're still on target for the day.

Desserts and snacks are always optional, and the serving sizes are on the smaller side so you can enjoy a few bites of something indulgent without going over in carbs or your macros.

Week 1 is all about easing you into your new keto diabetic meal plan. Don't be daunted by the shopping list. It is a long list because there are many keto-specific products that you'll need to have on hand, not just for this week but for the rest of the weeks, too.

This week focuses on dishes that are simple but still hearty and satisfying. And, like the other three weeks, you'll find a diverse selection of meals, all perfectly aligned with a keto diet to help keep you on target.

Breakfast will help you get your day started the right way. This week you can enjoy one of my all-time favorites, Corned Beef Hash (page 46), plus savory Sausage and Cheese Egg Muffins (page 45). Both are quick fixes, and the egg muffins are perfect on those mornings when you need to dash out the door. If you want to make the Sausage and Cheese Egg Muffins ahead of time, go ahead. I've provided some tips for you in the Prep Ahead section.

We're going retro with a wedge salad for lunch this week but jazzing it up with an herb-filled creamy Italian dressing. Switch things up with a fun soup filled with meatballs and zucchini noodles, the long, thin, noodle-like strands of zucchini that you can make with a spiralizer. No spiralizer? No problem. Check the produce section of your grocery store for already prepped zucchini noodles, or use a vegetable peeler to make wide strips of pappardelle-like noodles.

Dinners this week are also designed to be a bit easier to prepare until you get accustomed to your new keto way of eating. You can look forward to a fabulous meal of Chicken Broccoli Alfredo (page 119), meaty Southern Smothered Pork Chops (page 142), and a fun and tasty Bacon Cheeseburger Skillet (page 144).

You'll also find a selection of snacks and desserts to hold you over between meals or to finish your meal with something special. These are always optional, so don't feel like you need to eat them if you're not hungry.

Prep Ahead

Equipment: You'll need a muffin tin and a spiralizer or peeler for the zucchini noodles. The suggested snacks for this week are all perfect for grab-and-go snacking. A kitchen scale will help you get an accurate serving, or use the nutrition label on the packages to help you. One thing I like to do is pre-portion the snacks and store them in small containers. That way I can just grab a container and not be tempted by an extra handful.

Recipe Prep: This is an easy week as far as cooking goes. Here are a few things you can do in advance if you have some time:

- Make the meatballs for the Meatball and Zucchini Noodle Soup (page 64).

- Or, make the entire soup ahead of time. Just keep the zucchini noodles separate; the soup will keep in the fridge for the week.

- The Sausage and Cheese Egg Muffins (page 45) are another tasty meal that can be prepped ahead of time. Make them as the recipe is written, then cool them before putting them into the fridge. They will be an easy grab-and-go breakfast.

- Make the Creamy Italian Dressing for the Wedge Salad (page 58) for lunch this week.

- If you've got meats in the freezer, put them in the fridge to defrost.

- You're going to need crispy bacon twice this week. You could fry it up ahead of time and pop it into the fridge until you need it.

Cauliflower rice can be made ahead of time, and you'll need this for the Tabbouleh (page 66). If you are making it yourself, core the cauliflower, break it into chunks, and pulse it in a food processor until it is coarse and grainy, similar to rice.

If you buy whole heads of broccoli for the Chicken Broccoli Alfredo (page 119), you can prep the broccoli ahead of time by cutting it into bite-size florets and chunks. Store these in the fridge until you're ready to make the dish.

Pre-portion your snacks. Weigh them (or use the nutrition label to help) and package portions so they're ready to go.

Ice cream. Yes, there's Easy No-Churn Keto Vanilla Ice Cream (page 154) for dessert this week. It is the perfect dish to make ahead and keep in the freezer until dessert time.

Shopping List

PANTRY

- Almond flour, superfine (¼ cup)
- Almonds (½ cup)
- Baking powder (½ teaspoon)
- Broth, beef, low-sodium (4½ cups)
- Broth, chicken, low-sodium (½ cup)
- Canned corned beef (12-ounce can)
- Chocolate chips, dark, sugar-free (2 tablespoons)
- Cocoa powder, unsweetened (2 tablespoons)
- Ketchup, sugar-free (2 tablespoons)
- Mayonnaise (¼ cup)
- Nonstick cooking spray
- Oil, avocado (2 tablespoons)
- Oil, olive, extra-virgin (½ cup)
- Pickles, dill (½ cup)
- Sugar substitute, granulated white (2 tablespoons)
- Sugar substitute, powdered (3 tablespoons)
- Tomatoes, canned, diced (15-ounce can)
- Vanilla extract, pure (½ teaspoon)
- Vinegar, white wine (2 tablespoons)

HERBS AND SPICES

- Garlic powder (½ teaspoon)
- Garlic salt (½ teaspoon)
- Italian seasoning (3 tablespoons)
- Salt, kosher (2½ teaspoons)
- Pepper, black (1½ teaspoons)

PRODUCE

- Cauliflower, riced (3 cups)
- Cucumber, English (1 cup)
- Garlic (3 cloves)
- Iceberg lettuce (1 head)
- Lemon juice (2 tablespoons)
- Mushrooms, white (8 ounces)
- Onion, red (¼ cup)
- Onion, yellow (1 cup)
- Parsley (¼ cup)
- Radishes (1 cup)
- Scallions (½ cup)
- Tomatoes, diced (1 cup)
- Tomatoes, grape (1 pint)
- Zucchini noodles (2 cups)

EGGS, DAIRY, AND DAIRY ALTERNATIVES

- Butter, salted (5 tablespoons)
- Cheese, Cheddar, sharp, grated (1½ cups)
- Cheese, parmesan, grated (¾ cup)
- Cream cheese (6 ounces)
- Cream, heavy whipping (4½ cups)
- Eggs, large (10)

FROZEN

- Broccoli, frozen (16-ounce bag)

MEAT/DELI

- Bacon slices (10)
- Breakfast sausage (½ pound)
- Chicken, breast, boneless, skinless (1 pound)
- Ground beef, lean (1½ pounds)
- Pork, chops, boneless (1 to 1½ pounds)
- Salami (5 ounces)

WEEK 1 MENU

	BREAKFAST	LUNCH	SNACK (OPTIONAL)	DINNER	DESSERT (OPTIONAL)
MONDAY	Sausage and Cheese Egg Muffins (page 45)	Wedge Salad with Creamy Italian Dressing (page 58)	1 ounce salami, 1 ounce Cheddar cheese	Chicken Broccoli Alfredo (page 119)	Chocolate Mug Cake (page 151)
TUESDAY	Corned Beef Hash (page 46)	Meatball and Zucchini Noodle Soup (page 64)	¼ cup almonds	Bacon Cheeseburger Skillet (page 144)	Easy No-Churn Keto Vanilla Ice Cream (page 154)
WEDNESDAY	Sausage and Cheese Egg Muffins (leftover)	Wedge Salad with Creamy Italian Dressing (leftover)	1 ounce salami, 1 ounce Cheddar cheese	Chicken Broccoli Alfredo (leftover)	Chocolate Mug Cake (leftover)
THURSDAY	Corned Beef Hash (leftover)	Tabbouleh (page 66)	¼ cup almonds, 1 ounce Cheddar cheese	Southern Smothered Pork Chops (page 142)	Easy No-Churn Keto Vanilla Ice Cream (leftover)
FRIDAY	Sausage and Cheese Egg Muffins (leftover)	Meatball and Zucchini Noodle Soup (leftover)	2 ounces salami, 1 ounce Cheddar cheese	Bacon Cheeseburger Skillet (leftover)	Chocolate Mug Cake (leftover)
SATURDAY	Corned Beef Hash (leftover)	Tabbouleh (leftover)	¼ cup almonds, 1 ounce Cheddar cheese	Southern Smothered Pork Chops (leftover)	Easy No-Churn Keto Vanilla Ice Cream (leftover)
SUNDAY	Sausage and Cheese Egg Muffin (leftover)	Meatball and Zucchini Noodle Soup (leftover)	1 ounce salami, 1 ounce Cheddar cheese	Chicken Broccoli Alfredo (leftover)	Chocolate Mug Cake (leftover)

WEEK 2

About the Plan

Congratulations! You've finished your first week with your new keto meal plan. I hope you enjoyed your meals and came to realize that keto food can be delicious.

This week, we will introduce new ingredients and flavors. The recipes are still manageable and straightforward, and you still won't be spending hours in the kitchen. For breakfast this week, you can look forward to crunchy Keto Granola (page 50). Pair your granola with almond milk to keep the carbs in check. Also on the menu for breakfast this week is a thick and creamy Strawberry Smoothie (page 44). And, to keep breakfast quick and easy, I've got some great tips for you in the Prep Ahead section.

Lunch this week includes a delicious twist on chicken salad. Chicken and Avocado Salad (page 60) is meaty, creamy, and loaded with healthy fats. Once cut, avocados don't keep long, so add the avocado right before eating. Alternate the salad with a hearty serving of Unstuffed Pepper Soup (page 67). This keto classic is filled with savory beef, peppers, and a slurpable broth. And, for even more variety, you can enjoy my famous egg salad (page 63). Served in lettuce cups (or eat it with a fork), I've been making the egg salad this way for decades.

You'll look forward to dinner this week with retro classics: Cheesy Tuna Casserole (page 99) and Salisbury Steak (page 138). Love shrimp? You're in luck this week because Shrimp in Cajun Cream Sauce with Zucchini Noodles (page 106) is also on the menu. This is one of my favorites. It's so creamy, and it has a nice bold kick of spice to it. And one more: Garlic Butter Chicken with Cauliflower Rice (page 126) is so good and it makes perfect lunches, too, if you're tired of soups and salads.

Are you craving a snack? This week's snacks include a variety of easy-to-make picks and grab-and-go snacks. The Keto Chili Snack Mix (page 55) is perfect for portioning ahead of time, and pork rinds with cream cheese is a crunchy and creamy snack that's totally keto.

For dessert this week, enjoy Cheesecake Fluff with Raspberries and Almonds (page 153) or Crème Brûlée (page 156). The fluff is light, airy, and perfectly decadent, and the crème brûlée is a deceptively easy dessert that's indulgent while still being low in net carbs; you'll need small ramekins to make it. If you have a culinary torch to caramelize the sweetener on the top of the brûlée, great. Otherwise, I'll give you instructions on how to do it under your broiler.

Prep Ahead

Equipment: You're going to do some baking this week, so a hand mixer (or stand mixer) will come in handy, as will baking sheets. If you have parchment paper handy, it'll help make cleanup a breeze. Line the baking sheet with parchment paper before baking the Keto Snack Mix.

Recipe Prep: This week's recipes are a wee bit more complicated than last week's, but they are still within reach of novice cooks. You can get a good start to Week 2 with a bit of prep, if you have time.

- Make the granola ahead of time (page 50). Store it in an airtight container in your pantry or on your counter for quick and easy morning meals.

- Make prep easy for yourself this week and pick up a rotisserie chicken to make the Chicken and Avocado Salad (page 60). Avocados don't keep well once cut, but you can dice the chicken to get it ready for the salad. Add the avocados right before serving to keep them bright and green. Only use enough avocado for one serving; that way, you can enjoy the leftovers later in the week.

- For the Egg Salad in Lettuce Cups (page 63), hard-boil the eggs and chill them ahead of time so the salad comes together quickly. My foolproof method for making perfect hard-boiled eggs is to put the eggs in cold water in a pot. Put the pot on to boil over high heat and boil for 7 minutes. Turn the heat off and put a lid on the eggs. Don't peek for 10 minutes. Then, cool the eggs under cold running water and peel them.

- This week's soup, Unstuffed Pepper Soup (page 67), can also be made ahead if you have time.

- For dinners, you'll need cauliflower rice again—and by now you should be a pro. Make it yourself to keep the costs down, or, if you're short on time, buy it already riced. Zucchini noodles are also on the menu, and they can be spiralized ahead of time, too.

- You can also make the sweets for this week ahead of time. Both the Cheesecake Fluff with Raspberries and Almonds (page 153) and the Crème Brûlée (page 156) can be made at the beginning of the week and enjoyed for dessert. The Keto Chili Snack Mix (page 55) is an easy one to make ahead. Make a double batch and you'll have enough to nibble on later, too. It'll keep for a week or more. Portion it, too, so you're not tempted to eat more than you should.

You'll also need 3 hard-boiled eggs this week—those are perfect for prepping ahead of time.

Shopping List

PANTRY

- Almonds, slivered (1¼ cups)
- Broth, beef, low-sodium (5 cups)
- Broth, chicken, low-sodium (½ cup)
- Cheese snacks, baked (½ cup)
- Coconut, unsweetened, shredded (1 cup)
- Maple syrup, sugar-free (⅓ cup)
- Mayonnaise (4 tablespoons)
- Mustard, Dijon (4 teaspoons)

- Oil, avocado (2 tablespoons)
- Pecans, chopped (1 cup)
- Pecans, halves (½ cup)
- Pepper, black (1¼ teaspoons)
- Pork rinds (3 ounces)
- Pumpkin seeds (½ cup)
- Salt, kosher (3 ½ teaspoons)
- Sesame seeds (¼ cup)
- Sugar substitute, powdered (⅓ cup)

- Sugar substitute, white, granulated (½ cup plus ½ teaspoon)
- Sunflower seeds (¼ cup)
- Tomato paste (2 teaspoons)
- Tomatoes, canned, diced (15-ounce can)
- Tuna, canned, water-packed (2 [5-ounce] cans)
- Vanilla extract, pure (¾ teaspoon)
- Worcestershire sauce (1 teaspoon)

HERBS AND SPICES

- Cajun seasoning (1 tablespoon)
- Chili Powder (1 tablespoon)

- Everything Bagel Seasoning (¾ teaspoon)

- Garlic powder (¾ teaspoon)

- Italian seasoning (1 tablespoon + ¼ teaspoon)
- Paprika (¼ teaspoon)
- Xanthan gum (¼ teaspoon)

PRODUCE

- Avocado (1)
- Cauliflower rice (5 cups)
- Celery (½ cup)
- Cilantro (2 tablespoons)
- Garlic (2 cloves)
- Lemon, juice (1½ tablespoons)
- Lettuce, romaine (1 head)
- Lime, juice (1 tablespoon)
- Onions, yellow (½ cup)
- Parsley (3 tablespoons, plus more for garnish, optional)
- Peppers, bell, green (2 cups)
- Raspberries (½ cup)
- Scallions (¼ cup plus 2 tablespoons, plus more for garnish, optional)
- Tomatoes, diced (optional, for garnish)
- Zucchini (1 pound)
- Zucchini noodles (2 cups)

EGGS, DAIRY, AND DAIRY ALTERNATIVES

- Butter, salted (¾ cup plus 2 tablespoons)
- Cheese, Cheddar, shredded (1½ cups)
- Cream cheese (10 ounces)
- Cream, heavy whipping (4 cups)
- Eggs, large (16)
- Milk, almond (1½ cups)
- Sour cream (4 tablespoons)
- Strawberries, frozen (½ cup)

MEAT/DELI

- Beef, ground, lean (1½ pounds)
- Chicken, breast, boneless, skinless (1 pound)
- Chicken, cooked and shredded (2 cups)
- Shrimp, large, peeled and deveined (1 pound)

WEEK 2 MENU

	BREAKFAST	LUNCH	SNACK (OPTIONAL)	DINNER	DESSERT (OPTIONAL)
MONDAY	Keto Granola (page 50)	Unstuffed Pepper Soup (page 67)	1 hard-boiled egg with ¼ tsp Everything Bagel Seasoning	Cheesy Tuna Casserole (page 99)	Cheesecake Fluff with Raspberries and Almonds (page 153)
TUESDAY	Strawberry Smoothie (page 44)	Chicken and Avocado Salad (page 60)	Keto Chili Snack Mix (page 55)	Salisbury Steak (page 138)	Crème Brûlée (page 156)
WEDNESDAY	*Keto Granola (leftover)*	*Unstuffed Pepper Soup (leftover)*	1 hard-boiled egg with ¼ tsp Everything Bagel Seasoning	*Cheesy Tuna Casserole (leftover)*	*Cheesecake Fluff with Raspberries and Almonds (leftover)*
THURSDAY	*Strawberry Smoothie (leftover)*	Egg Salad in Lettuce Cups (page 63)	1 ounce pork rinds + 2 tablespoons cream cheese	*Salisbury Steak (leftover)*	*Crème Brûlée (leftover)*
FRIDAY	*Keto Granola (leftover)*	*Unstuffed Pepper Soup (leftover)*	1 hard-boiled egg with ¼ tsp Everything Bagel Seasoning	Shrimp in Cajun Cream Sauce with Zucchini Noodles (page 106)	*Cheesecake Fluff with Raspberries and Almonds (leftover)*
SATURDAY	*Strawberry Smoothie (leftover)*	*Egg Salad in Lettuce Cups (leftover)*	1 ounce pork rinds + 2 tablespoons cream cheese	Garlic Butter Chicken with Cauliflower Rice (page 126)	*Crème Brûlée (leftover)*
SUNDAY	Keto Granola (leftover)	*Garlic Butter Chicken with Cauliflower Rice (leftover)*	*Keto Chili Snack Mix (leftover)*	*Shrimp in Cajun Cream Sauce with Zucchini Noodles (leftover)*	*Cheesecake Fluff with Raspberries and Almonds (leftover)*

WEEK 3

About the Plan

By now you're practically a keto pro. Over time you'll start to know what's a good keto ingredient and what isn't—and you'll know approximately how many net carbs are in each. You're well on your way to mastering your keto lifestyle.

There are more delicious recipes coming your way this week, and, like the previous weeks, each is designed to minimize your time in the kitchen while maximizing flavor. This meal plan is also fluid, so mix and match or swap the recipes around to enjoy all your favorites.

This week you can look forward to Baked Avocado Boats with Eggs (page 47) and Blueberry Muffins (page 49) for breakfast. Yes, muffins can be keto. Light, fluffy, and delicious muffins are the perfect grab-and-go breakfast. The Baked Avocado Boats with Eggs are creamy and delicious if you've got a bit more time in the mornings. And, in case you're getting tired of reading recipes, you can take a break with a simple breakfast of sausage and eggs. Just keep an eye on the ingredients label on sausages—hidden sugars and starches can inflate your carb count.

For lunch, we're jazzing up tuna salad. The Tex-Mex Tuna Salad (page 61) is popping with flavor. Turn a humble can of tuna into something amazing. Alternate with the Italian Vegetable Soup with Sausage (page 68). This hearty soup is packed full of fiber-rich veggies, and you can even add more vegetables to it. There are tips on how to do this in the recipe. And one more soup for you this week: Chicken Enchilada Soup (page 70). I have a particular fondness for soups and this one is a winner. It's so chunky and packed with flavor, I know you'll love it.

Dinners this week are especially delicious, and I've got a few tasty twists on classics for you. Chicken Parmesan (page 122) and Beef Stroganoff Casserole (page 136) are joined by a hearty Cauliflower and Broccoli Bake (page 84). Each dish is hearty, delicious, and not that hard to make.

Mini Strawberry Cheesecakes (page 150) and Peanut Butter Cookie Dough Fat Bombs (page 152) are your sweets for the week. Both are easy to make but still indulgent enough to feel like real treats.

Your snacks this week include Deviled Eggs with Bacon (page 52). Bacon transforms this easy snack into a delicious treat, and for an easy grab-and-go option, try the roasted nuts and cheese. Pair your favorite cheese with the crunchy nuts for a satisfying snack.

Prep Ahead

Equipment: In Week 3, you'll need a regular-size 12-cup muffin tin, and your baking sheets and parchment paper will come in handy when making the Peanut Butter Cookie Dough Fat Bombs.

Recipe Prep:

The Blueberry Muffins (page 49) only need to be baked once, and, once cooled, they'll keep in the fridge for a few days. Or freeze them to keep them fresh for longer.

Boil the eggs ahead of time to make the Deviled Eggs with Bacon (page 52), then pop them into the fridge in an airtight container. Or make the whole recipe—they'll keep covered in the fridge for the week.

Peanut Butter Cookie Dough Fat Bombs (page 152) will keep in the fridge or freezer, making them a great pick to prep ahead of time.

This week's soup, Italian Vegetable Soup with Sausage (page 68), is another recipe that you can make ahead of time. Just keep it in the fridge and eat it for lunches during the week. It also makes a great low net carb snack—heat a mugful and enjoy.

Save some time throughout the week and get all the slicing and dicing out of the way now. Prep the cauliflower and broccoli, slice the onions, and prep the mushrooms ahead of time, then keep them in separate airtight containers in the fridge until you need them.

Shopping List

PANTRY

Almond flour, super-fine (4¼ cups)

Baking powder (1½ teaspoons)

Baking soda (1 teaspoon)

Broth, beef, low-sodium (½ cup)

Broth, chicken, low-sodium (8 cups)

Marinara sauce, sugar-free (1½ cups)

Mayonnaise (2 tablespoons)

Mustard, Dijon (1 tablespoon plus 1 teaspoon)

Oil, avocado (¼ cup plus 1 tablespoon)

- Oil, olive, extra-virgin (¼ teaspoon)
- Peanut butter, natural (2 tablespoons)
- Pecans, roasted (¾ cup)
- Pepper, black (¼ teaspoon)
- Salt, kosher (2¼ teaspoons)
- Sugar substitute, white, granulated (1¼ cups)
- Tomatoes, canned, diced, fire-roasted (15-ounce can)
- Tuna, canned (2 [5-ounce] cans)
- Vanilla extract (1½ teaspoons)

HERBS AND SPICES

- Chipotle powder (½ teaspoon)
- Italian seasoning (1 tablespoon)
- Taco seasoning (2 tablespoons)

EGGS, DAIRY, AND DAIRY ALTERNATIVES

- Butter, salted (2 sticks)
- Cheese, any kind (3 ounces))
- Cheese, Cheddar, shredded (2½ cups)
- Cheese, mozzarella, shredded (2 cups)
- Cheese, parmesan, grated (1 cup)
- Cream cheese (18 ounces)
- Cream, heavy whipping (4 cups)
- Eggs, large (24)
- Sour cream (1 tablespoon)

PRODUCE

- Avocados (2)
- Basil (1 bunch)
- Blueberries (1 cup)
- Broccoli florets (3 cups)
- Carrots (½ cup)
- Cauliflower florets (3 cups)
- Celery, diced (½ cup)
- Chives (1 bunch, optional, for garnish)
- Cilantro (2 tablespoons)
- Garlic, cloves (4)

- Kale (2 cups)
- Lemon juice (2 teaspoons)
- Lime juice (2 tablespoons)
- Mushrooms, white (1 pound)
- Onion and bell pepper blend, diced, frozen (1 cup)
- Onion, yellow (¾ cup)
- Parsley (1 bunch, optional, for garnish)
- Pepper, bell, red, diced (¼ cup)
- Pepper, jalapeño (1 tablespoon)
- Scallions (¼ cup)
- Strawberries, sliced (½ cup)
- Tomatoes, cherry (2 cups)

MEAT/DELI

- Bacon, sliced (10)
- Beef, ground, lean (1 pound)
- Chicken, breasts, boneless, skinless (1 pound)
- Chicken, cooked (1 cup)
- Sausage, breakfast links (12 links)
- Sausage, Italian (½ pound)

WEEK 3 MENU

	BREAKFAST	LUNCH	SNACK (OPTIONAL)	DINNER	DESSERT (OPTIONAL)
MONDAY	Baked Avocado Boats with Eggs (page 47)	Tex-Mex Tuna Salad (page 61)	Deviled Eggs with Bacon (page 52)	Cauliflower and Broccoli Bake (page 84)	Mini Strawberry Cheesecakes (page 150)
TUESDAY	Baked Avocado Boats with Eggs (page 47)	Italian Vegetable Soup with Sausage (page 68)	¼ cup roasted pecans, 1 ounce cheese	Chicken Parmesan (page 122)	Peanut Butter Cookie Dough Fat Bomb (page 152)
WEDNESDAY	2 scrambled eggs, 4 breakfast sausage links	Tex-Mex Tuna Salad (leftover)	Deviled Eggs with Bacon (leftover)	Cauliflower and Broccoli Bake (leftover)	Mini Strawberry Cheesecakes (leftover)
THURSDAY	Blueberry Muffins (page 49)	Italian Vegetable Soup with Sausage (leftover)	¼ cup roasted pecans, 1 ounce cheese	Chicken Parmesan (leftover)	Peanut Buter Cookie Dough Fat Bomb (leftover)
FRIDAY	2 scrambled eggs, 4 breakfast sausage links	Chicken Enchilada Soup (page 70)	Deviled Eggs with Bacon (leftover)	Beef Stroganoff Casserole (page 136)	Mini Strawberry Cheesecakes (leftover)
SATURDAY	Blueberry Muffins (leftover)	Italian Vegetable Soup with Sausage (leftover)	¼ cup roasted pecans, 1 ounce cheese	Chicken Parmesan (leftover)	Peanut Buter Cookie Dough Fat Bomb (leftover)
SUNDAY	2 scrambled eggs, 4 breakfast sausage links	Chicken Enchilada Soup (leftover)	Deviled Eggs with Bacon (leftover)	Beef Stroganoff Casserole (leftover)	Mini Strawberry Cheesecakes (leftover)

WEEK 4

About the Plan

Welcome to week 4. You're almost a month in. You have one more week of fabulous recipes to see you on your way to a keto lifestyle. These are delicious recipes, but you can also swap them out with one of the other recipes in the book. Just adjust your daily macros or make sure you're under 20 net carbs per day.

For breakfast this week, dig into a keto-ized classic: Avocado Toast (page 48) on a light and crispy chaffle instead of carb-heavy bread. This meal is alternated with Chorizo Baked Eggs (page 51), which is a tasty twist on shakshuka, a popular Middle Eastern dish. And, for more variety, bacon and eggs. Fried, poached, scrambled—it's up to you.

This week, there are three delicious recipes for lunch: a hearty BLT Salad (page 62) that's loaded with crispy bacon, thick and rich Broccoli and Cheddar Soup (page 69), and a Greek Salad (page 59) with tangy feta cheese. I love the crispy freshness of the Greek Salad, and that soup is better than any starch-thickened restaurant soup.

For dinners this week, the Sausage and Rapini Bake (page 145) is meaty, creamy, and so satisfying. Rapini, also known as broccoli rabe, is a leafy green with a bit of bitterness to it. If you can't find it, though it is widely available in most produce sections of grocery stores, you can substitute broccolini or even regular broccoli. The Asparagus Frittata (page 74) is a lighter pick for this week, and the Ground Beef and Cauliflower (page 143) has delicious Asian flavors.

For sweets this week, treat yourself to creamy Peanut Butter Mousse (page 155) and Chocolate Nut Clusters (page 158). Grab-and-go snack options include pepperoni slices, pork rinds, and celery with cream cheese. Sprinkle some Everything Bagel seasoning on the cream cheese for even more flavor.

Prep Ahead

Equipment:
You'll need a hand mixer or stand mixer for the Peanut Butter Mousse (page 155) and a mini waffle maker to make the chaffles. A baking sheet and parchment paper will help keep the Chocolate Nut Clusters (page 158) from sticking to the pan while they cool and set.

Recipe Prep:

- Chaffles (page 48) are easy to make ahead, and they'll keep in the fridge for a week. You can also freeze the chaffles. To reheat them, pop them back into the mini waffle maker for a few minutes to get toasty, or warm them in your toaster oven or regular oven.

- You can fry the bacon ahead of time for the BLT Salad (page 62), and you can also pre-chop the scallions for this recipe.

- If you have time to chop and slice, wash and trim the celery, rapini, and asparagus for the Sausage and Rapini Bake (page 145) and snacks. These veggies will keep well in the fridge for a few days until you're ready to cook with them. This week's desserts are also great picks to prep ahead of time. The Peanut Butter Mousse (page 155) will keep nicely in the fridge and the Chocolate Nut Clusters (page 158) are best kept in an airtight container on the counter.

Shopping List

PANTRY

- Almond flour, super-fine (4¼ cups)
- Broth, beef, low-sodium (¼ cup)
- Broth, chicken, low-sodium (3¼ cups)
- Chocolate chips, dark, sugar-free (¼ cup)
- Coconut aminos (2 tablespoons)
- Mayonnaise (2 tablespoons)
- Mustard powder (½ teaspoon)
- Nuts, mixed (¾ cup)
- Oil, avocado (¼ cup plus 3 tablespoons)
- Oil, coconut (½ teaspoon)
- Oil, olive, extra-virgin (¼ cup)
- Olives, sliced (¼ cup)
- Peanut butter (¼ cup)
- Pepper, black (½ teaspoon)
- Pork rinds (4 ounces)
- Salt, kosher (1¾ teaspoons)
- Sesame seeds (½ teaspoon)
- Sugar substitute, powdered (3 tablespoons)
- Tomatoes, diced (15-ounce can)
- Vinegar, red wine (2 tablespoons)

HERBS AND SPICES

- Oregano, dried (½ tablespoon)
- Paprika (1 teaspoon)

EGGS, DAIRY, AND DAIRY ALTERNATIVES

- Butter, salted (2 tablespoons)
- Cheese (1 ounce)
- Cheese, Cheddar, shredded (2 cups)
- Cheese, feta, crumbled (4 ounces)
- Cheese, Jarlsberg, shredded (1 cup)
- Cheese, mozzarella, shredded (1 cup)
- Cheese, parmesan, grated (½ cup)
- Cheese, ricotta (½ cup)
- Cream cheese (13 ounces)
- Cream, heavy whipping (2¼ cups)
- Eggs, large (16)
- Sour cream (2 tablespoons)

PRODUCE

- Asparagus (1 pound)
- Avocados (2)
- Broccoli (4 cups)
- Cauliflower (4 cups)
- Celery (1 bunch)
- Chives (1 tablespoon)
- Cucumber, English (3 cups)
- Garlic, cloves (4)
- Ginger (1 tablespoon)
- Lemon, juice (1 tablespoon)
- Lettuce (6 cups)
- Lime, juice (2 teaspoons)
- Onions, yellow, diced (1 cup)
- Peppers, bell, green, diced (½ cup)
- Rapini/broccoli rabe (1 bunch)
- Scallions (¾ cup)
- Tomatoes, grape (2 cups)

MEAT/DELI

- Bacon, sliced (12)
- Beef, ground, lean (1 pound)
- Chicken, breast, boneless, skinless (1 pound)
- Pepperoni, sliced (3 ounces)
- Sausage, chorizo (½ pound)
- Sausage, Italian (1 pound)

WEEK 4 MENU

	BREAKFAST	LUNCH	SNACK (OPTIONAL)	DINNER	DESSERT (OPTIONAL)
MONDAY	Avocado Toast on Crispy Chaffles (page 48)	BLT Salad (page 62)	2 celery stalks with 3 tablespoons cream cheese	Sausage and Rapini Bake (page 145)	Peanut Butter Mousse (page 155)
TUESDAY	*Avocado Toast on Crispy Chaffles (leftover)*	Broccoli and Cheddar Soup (page 69)	1 ounce pepperoni slices	Asparagus Frittata (page 74)	Chocolate Nut Clusters (page 158)
WEDNESDAY	Chorizo Baked Eggs (page 51)	*BLT Salad (leftover)*	2 celery stalks with 3 tablespoons cream cheese	*Sausage and Rapini Bake (leftover)*	*Peanut Butter Mousse (leftover)*
THURSDAY	Bacon and Eggs (2 fried eggs, 4 strips crispy bacon)	*Broccoli and Cheddar Soup (leftover)*	1 ounce pepperoni slices	*Asparagus Frittata (leftover)*	*Chocolate Nut Clusters (leftover)*
FRIDAY	*Chorizo Baked Eggs (leftover)*	Greek Salad (page 59)	2 ounces pork rinds	Ground Beef and Cauliflower (page 143)	*Peanut Butter Mousse (leftover)*
SATURDAY	Bacon and Eggs (2 fried eggs, 4 strips crispy bacon)	*Greek Salad (leftover)*	1 ounce pepperoni and 1 ounce cheese	*Sausage and Rapini Bake (leftover)*	*Chocolate Nut Clusters (leftover)*
SUNDAY	*Chorizo Baked Eggs (leftover)*	*Greek Salad (leftover)*	2 ounces pork rinds	*Ground Beef and Cauliflower (leftover)*	*Peanut Butter Mousse (leftover)*

AVOCADO TOAST ON CRISPY CHAFFLES, PAGE 48

CHAPTER THREE

Breakfast and Snacks

START YOUR DAY WITH SOMETHING delicious that's well balanced and in line with your keto meal plan. There are fruity picks (yes, some fruit is okay on keto), meaty dishes, and egg-centric ones. From smoothies and muffins to skillets and more—rev up your appetite and cook something fabulous today. With a variety of quick fixes and dishes that take a little bit more time, there's something for every day of the week in this section.

Strawberry Smoothie

PREP TIME: 2 minutes | **SERVES 1**

Sweet, creamy, and delicious, there's nothing like a thick and rich smoothie to get your day off to a great start. Are you tired of strawberries? Mix it up with other keto-friendly berries like raspberries or blueberries.

½ cup unsweetened almond milk

½ cup frozen strawberries, partially thawed

¼ cup heavy cream

½ teaspoon granulated white sugar substitute

2 or 3 ice cubes

1. Put the almond milk, strawberries, cream, sugar substitute, and ice cubes into a blender, pulse it 3 to 4 times, then scrape down the sides with a spatula. Continue pulsing until it is all blended.

2. Pour the smoothie into a glass and enjoy.

VARIATION: Make this smoothie dairy-free by substituting coconut milk for the heavy cream.

MACRONUTRIENTS: 77% Fat, 4% Protein, 19% Carbs

PER SERVING: Calories: 280; Total fat: 24g; Saturated fat: 0g; Protein: 3g; Total carbohydrates: 13g; Fiber: 3g; Erythritol: 2g; Net carbs: 10g; Cholesterol: 0mg

GLUTEN-FREE | NUT-FREE | SOY-FREE

Sausage and Cheese Egg Muffins

PREP TIME: 10 minutes | **COOK TIME:** 23 minutes | **SERVES 4**

Cook it once and eat it four times with this tasty meal prep recipe. A quick and delicious breakfast, these yummy egg muffins heat up quickly in the microwave, making them a great grab-and-go morning meal.

Nonstick cooking spray

½ pound breakfast sausage, casings removed

8 large eggs

½ cup shredded Cheddar cheese

¼ cup sliced scallions, both white and green parts

¼ teaspoon kosher salt

¼ teaspoon freshly ground black pepper

MACRONUTRIENTS: 73% Fat, 25% Protein, 2% Carbs

1. Preheat the oven to 350°F and lightly spray 6 cups of a regular-size muffin tin with cooking spray.

2. In a medium skillet over medium heat, cook the breakfast sausage until there's no pink remaining, about 6 minutes. Drain any fat.

3. Whip the eggs with a fork or a whisk in a medium bowl until frothy and well mixed.

4. Add the cooked sausage, cheese, scallions, salt, and pepper to the eggs. Mix well.

5. Divide the egg and sausage mixture among the 6 muffin cups and bake for 15 to 17 minutes or until set in the middle.

6. Refrigerate the leftovers for up to 4 days in an airtight container. To reheat, simply wrap the egg muffin in a paper towel and heat for 20 seconds on HIGH in the microwave.

PREP TIP: Get creative and substitute cooked bacon crumbles or diced ham for the sausage, and use different cheeses like Swiss, Gouda, Monterey Jack, or pepper Jack.

PER SERVING: Calories: 399; Total fat: 32g; Saturated fat: 12g; Protein: 24g; Total carbohydrates: 2g; Fiber: 0g; Erythritol: 0g; Net carbs: 2g; Cholesterol: 429mg

Corned Beef Hash

PREP TIME: 5 minutes | **COOK TIME:** 12 minutes | **SERVES 4**

Traditionally made with plenty of potatoes and onions, this version of the deli classic gets a keto makeover. Radishes are a tasty and low-carb substitute for potatoes; dice them small, and you will never know they're not carb-loaded potatoes. Made easily with canned corned beef, this is a tasty breakfast recipe.

1 tablespoon avocado oil

1 (12-ounce) can corned beef

1 cup radishes, cut into ¼-inch dice

¼ teaspoon garlic powder

¼ teaspoon freshly ground black pepper

MACRONUTRIENTS: 71% Fat, 27% Protein, 2% Carbs

1. Heat the oil in a large skillet over medium-high heat until shimmering but not smoking.

2. Add the corned beef and radishes, using a spatula to break up the corned beef.

3. Cook over medium heat for 8 to 10 minutes, stirring occasionally, until the radishes are tender.

4. Turn the heat up to high and press the corned beef mixture down in the skillet. Cook for 1 to 2 minutes or until the corned beef gets crispy. Turn off the heat, season with the garlic powder and pepper, and serve.

5. Refrigerate the cooled leftovers in an airtight container for 4 to 5 days. To reheat, warm the corned beef hash in a small skillet over medium heat, or heat it in the microwave for 1 to 2 minutes or until warmed through.

VARIATION: Use 1 cup of cauliflower rice instead of the radishes, but reduce your cook time to about 6 minutes because the cauliflower will cook faster.

PER SERVING: Calories: 250; Total fat: 20g; Saturated fat: 6g; Protein: 16g; Total carbohydrates: 2g; Fiber: 1g; Erythritol: 0g; Net carbs: 1g; Cholesterol: 83mg

Baked Avocado Boats with Eggs

PREP TIME: 5 minutes | **COOK TIME:** 20 minutes | **SERVES 4**

This simple dish packs a powerful punch with oodles of flavor and plenty of good-for-you-fats, and with a creamy texture and a bit of crunchy bacon, it's perfect for breakfast or brunch.

2 ripe avocados, cut in half lengthwise and pitted
4 large eggs
Kosher salt
Freshly ground black pepper
4 slices bacon, chopped

MACRONUTRIENTS: 71% Fat, 18% Protein, 11% Carbs

1. Preheat the oven to 350°F.

2. Use a spoon to scoop out the avocado flesh to make the pit hollow bigger, large enough to hold the egg.

3. Crack an egg into the scooped-out hole of each avocado half.

4. Sprinkle the avocado halves with salt and pepper and place them on a baking sheet. Bake for about 20 minutes or until the eggs are set.

5. While the avocados bake, fry the bacon in a medium skillet over medium-high heat until crispy, about 6 minutes. Transfer the bacon with a slotted spoon to a sheet of paper towel to absorb the rest of the bacon fat.

6. Garnish the cooked avocado boats with the crispy bacon and enjoy.

7. Cover the cooled leftovers tightly with plastic wrap and store them in the fridge for up to 4 days. To reheat, warm them in the oven or reheat them in the microwave for 30 to 40 seconds on high.

PREP TIP: Use precooked bacon or real bacon bits instead of frying the bacon to make this dish even easier.

PER SERVING: Calories: 289; Total fat: 24g; Saturated fat: 5g; Protein: 12g; Total carbohydrates: 9g; Fiber: 7g; Erythritol: 0g; Net carbs: 2g; Cholesterol: 179mg

Avocado Toast on Crispy Chaffles

PREP TIME: 5 minutes | **COOK TIME:** 12 minutes | **SERVES 4**

A keto riff on the bistro classic, there's nothing like fresh and creamy avocado on a lightly toasted chaffle. Feel free to jazz up this recipe with fresh cilantro, bacon bits, Everything Bagel seasoning, or any of your favorite flavors.

Nonstick cooking spray

2 large egg whites

1 cup shredded mozzarella cheese

¼ cup superfine almond flour

2 avocados, cut in half lengthwise and pitted

2 teaspoons lime juice

⅛ teaspoon kosher salt

MACRONUTRIENTS: 71% Fat, 16% Protein, 13% Carbs

1. Heat a mini waffle maker per the manufacturer's instructions. Spray it lightly with nonstock cooking spray.

2. In a medium bowl, whip the egg whites with a fork until they are frothy. Mix in the shredded mozzarella cheese and the almond flour until well combined.

3. Add ¼ of the batter at a time to the waffle maker and cook until the chaffle is crispy and releases easily. Repeat with the remaining batter.

4. Meanwhile, mash the avocados with a fork in a small bowl. Add the lime juice and salt. Mix well.

5. To assemble, top each chaffle with ¼ of the avocado mixture and add your favorite toppings.

6. Put any leftover avocado mixture in a small bowl and cover with plastic wrap, pressing the plastic down to the surface of the avocado and pushing out any air bubbles. Refrigerate for up to 4 days. The chaffles can be kept in the fridge or freezer. Reheat the chaffles in a toaster or in the mini waffle maker.

PER SERVING: Calories: 288; Total fat: 24g; Saturated fat: 6g; Protein: 11g; Total carbohydrates: 10g; Fiber: 8g; Erythritol: 0g; Net carbs: 3g; Cholesterol: 22mg

Blueberry Muffins

PREP TIME: 10 minutes | **COOK TIME:** 20 minutes | **MAKES 12** muffins

Most traditional flours are a no-no on keto, thanks to high carbohydrates, but these tasty muffins are made with flour substitutes, and they're just as good as the real thing.

2½ cups superfine almond flour

⅓ cup white granular sugar substitute

1½ teaspoons baking powder

1 teaspoon baking soda

⅓ cup (about 5 tablespoons) melted salted butter

⅓ cup heavy cream

3 large eggs

2 teaspoons lemon juice

1 teaspoon pure vanilla extract

1 cup blueberries, fresh or frozen

MACRONUTRIENTS: 77% Fat, 11% Protein, 12% Carbs

1. Preheat the oven to 350°F and line a 12-cup muffin pan with paper liners.

2. In a medium bowl, combine the almond flour, sugar substitute, baking powder, and baking soda.

3. Add the melted butter, cream, eggs, lemon juice, and vanilla. Mix until combined.

4. Fold in the blueberries.

5. Divide the batter among the 12 muffin cups and bake for about 20 minutes or until an inserted toothpick comes out clean.

6. Refrigerate any leftovers for up to 3 days, or freeze them for up to 3 months.

VARIATION: Substitute other low-carb berries like chopped strawberries, raspberries, or blackberries for the blueberries.

PER SERVING (1 MUFFIN): Calories: 209; Total fat: 19g; Saturated fat: 6g; Protein: 6g; Total carbohydrates: 7g; Fiber: 3g; Erythritol: 5g; Net carbs: 4g; Cholesterol: 69mg

Keto Granola

PREP TIME: 10 minutes | **COOK TIME:** 20 minutes | **SERVES 4**

This easy granola is a quick and easy breakfast, perfectly crunchy and loaded with keto-friendly ingredients. It also makes a great on-the-go snack or topping for sugar-free yogurt.

1 cup slivered almonds

1 cup chopped pecans

1 cup shredded unsweetened coconut

½ cup pumpkin seeds

¼ cup sunflower seeds

¼ cup sesame seeds

⅓ cup sugar-free maple syrup

1 large egg white

MACRONUTRIENTS: 78% Fat, 11% Protein, 11% Carbs

1. Preheat the oven to 350°F. Line a baking sheet with parchment paper.

2. In a large bowl, mix the almonds, pecans, coconut, pumpkin seeds, sunflower seeds, and sesame seeds. Add the sugar-free maple syrup and mix well.

3. In a small bowl, whip the egg white with a fork until frothy. Mix the egg white into the nut and seed mixture.

4. Spread the mixture onto the baking sheet and bake for 20 minutes, stirring halfway through.

5. Let the mixture cool completely before serving.

6. Store the leftovers in an airtight container on the counter for up to a week.

VARIATION: Jazz up your granola with a ½ cup of dehydrated keto-friendly fruits (blueberries, strawberries, raspberries, and blackberries are all good choices), and serve this granola with almond milk to keep the carbs in check.

PER SERVING: Calories: 591; Total fat: 55g; Saturated fat: 11g; Protein: 17g; Total carbohydrates: 17g; Fiber: 10g; Erythritol: 3g; Net carbs: 7g; Cholesterol: 0mg

Chorizo Baked Eggs

PREP TIME: 15 minutes | **COOK TIME:** 20 minutes | **SERVES 4**

These eggs are perfect for breakfast or brunch with big, bold Spanish flavors and plenty of meaty goodness. They're hearty enough for lunch or dinner, too, and can easily be scaled to feed more people, making this an easy and impressive dish for entertaining guests.

1 tablespoon avocado oil

¼ cup diced yellow onions

½ pound chorizo sausage

1 (15-ounce) can diced tomatoes, undrained

1 teaspoon paprika

½ teaspoon kosher salt

4 large eggs

MACRONUTRIENTS: 71% Fat, 23% Protein, 6% Carbs

PREP TIP: Chorizo comes in various forms: sausage links, bulk sausage, and dried. This recipe works best with raw chorizo, and if you buy the links, squeeze the meat out of the sausage casing before using it.

1. Preheat the oven to 350°F.

2. Heat the oil in a medium oven-safe skillet over medium-high heat until hot but not smoking. Add the onions and cook for 4 to 5 minutes or until the onions are softened and translucent but not brown.

3. Add the chorizo sausage to the skillet and break it up with a spatula, cooking until it is no longer pink, about 5 minutes.

4. Add the diced tomatoes, paprika, and salt to the skillet and mix well. Bring the mixture to a simmer and cook for about 5 minutes, until thickened.

5. Use a spatula to create 4 wells in the tomato mixture. Carefully crack an egg into each well.

6. Bake for about 5 minutes, until the whites have set but the yolks are still runny.

7. To serve, dish up a spoonful of the tomato mixture with an egg and enjoy.

8. Refrigerate the cooled leftovers in an airtight container for up to 1 week. To reheat, warm the leftovers in a 300°F oven in an oven-safe dish until heated through.

PER SERVING: Calories: 381; Total fat: 30g; Saturated fat: 10g; Protein: 21g; Total carbohydrates: 6g; Fiber: 2g; Erythritol: 0g; Net carbs: 4g; Cholesterol: 236mg

DAIRY-
FREE

GLUTEN-
FREE

NUT-
FREE

Deviled Eggs with Bacon

PREP TIME: 5 minutes | **COOK TIME:** 17 minutes | **SERVES 4**

Creamy and with the salty crunch of smoky bacon, these deviled eggs are the perfect keto snack. Make a batch and keep them in your fridge, snacking on them whenever you've got a craving for something delicious.

2 slices bacon, finely
   chopped

4 large eggs

2 tablespoons mayonnaise

1 teaspoon Dijon mustard

Pinch kosher salt

Freshly ground black
   pepper

MACRONUTRIENTS: 79% Fat,
20% Protein, 1% Carbs

1. Heat a small skillet over medium-high heat and cook the bacon until browned, about 6 minutes. Remove the bacon from the skillet with a slotted spoon and set it aside on a paper towel–lined plate.

2. Meanwhile, put the whole eggs in a small pot filled with cold water. Bring the pot to a boil over high heat and gently boil the eggs for 7 minutes. Turn off the heat and put a lid on the pot. Let the pot sit for 10 minutes without removing the lid.

3. When the 10 minutes are up, drain the eggs and put them in cold water. When they are cool, peel the eggs and halve them lengthwise.

4. Scoop out the cooked egg yolks and put them in a small bowl, keeping the whites intact. Using a fork, mix the yolks, mayonnaise, Dijon mustard, salt, and pepper until creamy and smooth.

5. Spoon the yolk filling back into the egg whites, dividing it equally. Top with the crumbled bacon and enjoy.

6. Refrigerate the leftovers in an airtight container for 3 to 4 days.

PER SERVING: Calories: 172; Total fat: 15g; Saturated fat: 2g; Protein: 8g; Total carbohydrates: 1g; Fiber: 0g; Erythritol: 0g; Net carbs: 1g; Cholesterol: 189mg

Pepperoni Pizza Chaffles

PREP TIME: 5 minutes | **COOK TIME:** 20 minutes | **SERVES 4**

Light, crispy, and not eggy-tasting, Pizza Chaffles are the perfect keto snack. Make a batch of chaffles and keep them in the freezer for quick snacking. To make it even easier, freeze sugar-free pizza sauce in an ice cube tray, then thaw a cube of sauce when you want to enjoy this treat. One cube is enough to top a chaffle.

Nonstick cooking spray

2 large egg whites

2 cups shredded
mozzarella cheese,
divided

¼ cup superfine almond
flour

½ cup sugar-free pizza
sauce

4 ounces pepperoni slices
(about 20 slices)

MACRONUTRIENTS: 66% Fat,
26% Protein, 8% Carbs

1. Heat a mini waffle maker according to the man-ufacturer's instructions. Spray the insides with cooking spray.

2. In a medium bowl, whip the egg whites with a fork until they are frothy. Mix in 1 cup of the mozzarella cheese and the almond flour until well combined.

3. Spoon a quarter of the batter onto the hot waffle maker and close the lid. Cook for 3 to 4 minutes or until the chaffle is golden brown and releases easily. Repeat with the remaining batter.

4. Top a chaffle with 2 tablespoons of sugar-free pizza sauce, ¼ cup of mozzarella, and 1 ounce of pepperoni slices.

5. Pop the chaffles under the broiler for 2 to 3 minutes or until the cheese is melted and bub-bling. Enjoy.

6. Store the leftover chaffles in a zip-top plastic bag in the freezer for up to a month. The pizza toppings will keep in the fridge for a week.

PER SERVING: Calories: 379; Total fat: 28g; Saturated fat: 12g; Protein: 23g; Total carbohydrates: 9g; Fiber: 2g; Erythritol: 0g; Net carbs: 7g; Cholesterol: 74mg

Blueberry Fat Bombs

PREP TIME: 10 minutes, plus 30 minutes freezing time | **COOK TIME:** 5 minutes
SERVES 8

These fat bombs are creamy, flavorful bites of deliciousness. Perfect for whenever you're craving a bite of something sweet or when you need to get your fat macros up. Keep these fat bombs on hand in the freezer for quick and easy snacking.

½ cup fresh blueberries

8 ounces cream cheese, at room temperature

1 cup unsweetened shredded coconut, divided

⅓ cup powdered sugar substitute

1 teaspoon pure vanilla extract

MACRONUTRIENTS: 85% Fat, 6% Protein, 9% Carbs

1. Cook the blueberries in a small saucepan over medium-low heat until they've popped but haven't become all liquid, about 5 minutes.

2. In a medium bowl, beat the blueberries, cream cheese, ½ cup of coconut, powdered sugar substitute, and vanilla with an electric hand mixer on high speed until well blended.

3. Put the blueberry–cream cheese mixture in the freezer for about 30 minutes or until it is hard enough to roll into balls.

4. Roll the mixture into 8 balls and press each ball into the remaining coconut to cover.

5. Refrigerate until firm and enjoy.

6. Store leftover bombs in the freezer, letting each thaw for 5 minutes before enjoying a cool and creamy treat.

   VARIATION: Swap the blueberries for other keto-friendly berries like strawberries, raspberries, or blackberries.

PER SERVING: Calories: 139; Total fat: 13g; Saturated fat: 8g; Protein: 2g; Total carbohydrates: 4g; Fiber: 1g; Erythritol: 8g; Net carbs: 3g; Cholesterol: 31mg

Keto Chili Snack Mix

PREP TIME: 10 minutes | **COOK TIME:** 46 minutes | **SERVES 4**

Grab a baggie of this tasty Keto Snack Mix when you're on the go, or grab a handful to nibble on in between meals. Packed with protein and good fats, this is one snack mix you can feel good about eating.

½ cup slivered almonds

½ cup pecan halves

½ cup unsweetened shredded coconut

2 cups roughly chopped pork rinds

½ cup baked cheese snacks (such as Whisps Cheese Crisps)

4 tablespoons salted butter

1 tablespoon Worcestershire sauce

1 tablespoon chili powder

MACRONUTRIENTS: 78% Fat, 15% Protein, 7% Carbs

1. Preheat the oven to 225°F. Line a baking sheet with parchment paper.

2. In a large bowl, mix the almonds, pecans, coconut, pork rinds, and baked cheese snacks.

3. In a small bowl, melt the butter in the microwave for 30 to 60 seconds, then stir in the Worcestershire sauce and chili powder.

4. Drizzle the butter mixture over the snack mix and toss well to coat. Spread the mixture on the baking sheet and bake for 45 minutes, stirring every 15 minutes to bake evenly.

5. Remove the snack mix from the oven and let it cool on the baking sheet.

6. To store the snack mix, place the cooled mixture in an airtight container or zip-top plastic bag on the counter for up to a week.

PREP TIP: Add some sweetness to your snack mix by adding ½ cup of sugar-free baking chips (Lily's) to the cooled mixture.

PER SERVING: Calories: 451; Total fat: 39g; Saturated fat: 13g; Protein: 17g; Total carbohydrates: 8g; Fiber: 5g; Erythritol: 0g; Net carbs: 3g; Cholesterol: 56mg

BLT SALAD, PAGE 62

CHAPTER FOUR

Soups and Salads

PERFECT FOR LUNCH OR LIGHTER dinners, soups and salads are satisfying and delicious. I've included a terrific selection of both creamy and brothy soups, plus light and hearty salads, so there's truly something to tempt everyone in this chapter. Plus, many of these soups can be made ahead of time. I've often got a batch of soup in the fridge for quick meals and whenever I need a snack.

Wedge Salad with Creamy Italian Dressing

PREP TIME: 10 minutes | **SERVES 4**

Wedge salads have been a steakhouse classic for years, but when loaded with croutons and starch-heavy dressings, they can be a carb pitfall. I've lightened the carbs and put a bit of a twist on the wedge salad, introducing some new flavors that you're sure to love.

4 slices bacon, chopped

¼ cup mayonnaise

2 tablespoons white wine vinegar

2 tablespoons extra-virgin olive oil

1 tablespoon Italian seasoning

¼ teaspoon garlic powder

1 head iceberg lettuce

1 cup diced tomato

¼ cup thinly sliced red onion

¼ cup grated parmesan cheese

MACRONUTRIENTS: 85% Fat, 8% Protein, 7% Carbs

1. In a small skillet over medium-high heat, cook the bacon until crisp, about 5 minutes. Remove the bacon from the skillet with a slotted spoon and set it aside on a paper towel–lined plate.

2. Meanwhile, in a jar with a tightly fitting lid, combine the mayonnaise, white wine vinegar, olive oil, Italian seasoning, and garlic powder. Shake vigorously until well mixed.

3. Quarter the iceberg lettuce. Spoon 2 tablespoons of the dressing over the top of each wedge, and garnish evenly with the crispy bacon, tomato, red onion, and parmesan cheese.

4. To store the leftovers, wrap the lettuce wedges tightly in plastic wrap, and refrigerate for up to 3 days. The dressing will keep in an airtight container in the fridge for up to 1 week.

PER SERVING: Calories: 310; Total fat: 29g; Saturated fat: 4g; Protein: 6g; Total carbohydrates: 6g; Fiber: 2g; Erythritol: 0g; Net carbs: 4g; Cholesterol: 11mg

Greek Salad

PREP TIME: 10 minutes | **SERVES 4**

Fresh, flavorful, and light, this easy salad is perfect as an entrée for lunch or as a side dish with dinner. Packed with flavor and a fresh tangy vinaigrette and plenty of crunchy vegetables, the salad comes together quickly and is as pretty as it is tasty.

3 cups diced English cucumber

1 cup grape tomatoes, cut in half

4 ounces feta cheese, crumbled

½ cup diced green bell pepper

¼ cup sliced olives, drained

¼ cup extra-virgin olive oil

2 tablespoons red wine vinegar

½ tablespoon dried oregano

¼ teaspoon kosher salt

Pinch red pepper flakes

MACRONUTRIENTS: 80% Fat, 9% Protein, 11% Carbs

1. In a medium bowl, toss together the cucumber, tomatoes, feta, pepper, and olives. Set aside.

2. To make the dressing, in a small bowl, whisk the olive oil and vinegar with the oregano, salt, and red pepper flakes.

3. Toss the dressing with the vegetables and feta and serve.

4. Cover the leftovers tightly and refrigerate for up 4 days.

PER SERVING: Calories: 227; Total fat: 21g; Saturated fat: 2g; Protein: 5g; Total carbohydrates: 7g; Fiber: 2g; Erythritol: 0g; Net carbs: 5g Cholesterol: 25mg

Chicken and Avocado Salad

PREP TIME: 10 minutes | **SERVES 4**

This salad is easy, creamy, chunky, and oh so delicious. It's perfect as a light lunch or a midafternoon snack. You can whip up a batch of this protein-packed salad in no time. If you like spice, add some finely diced jalapeño to jazz it up even more.

1 ripe avocado, peeled, pitted, and cubed

2 tablespoons mayonnaise

2 tablespoons sour cream

1 tablespoon lime juice

½ teaspoon kosher salt

¼ teaspoon freshly ground black pepper

2 cups diced cooked chicken

¼ cup sliced scallions, white and green parts

¼ cup diced celery

2 tablespoons chopped fresh cilantro

MACRONUTRIENTS: 58% Fat, 34% Protein, 8% Carbs

1. In a medium bowl, combine the avocado, mayonnaise, sour cream, lime juice, salt, and pepper. Mix well, mashing the avocado slightly, but keep it chunky.

2. Add the chicken, scallions, and celery and toss well. Garnish with the chopped cilantro and serve immediately.

3. Wrap any leftovers in plastic wrap and refrigerate for up to 1 day.

PREP TIP: Leftover rotisserie chicken works well in this recipe, or purchase precooked chicken breast strips (unbreaded).

PER SERVING: Calories: 250; Total fat: 16g; Saturated fat: 3g; Protein: 20g; Total carbohydrates: 5g; Fiber: 4g; Erythritol: 0g; Net carbs: 1g; Cholesterol: 59mg

Tex-Mex Tuna Salad

PREP TIME: 10 minutes | **SERVES 4**

Are you tired of plain old tuna? Jazz up that canned tuna with big and bold Southwestern flavors. This easy salad goes great in a lettuce cup for a tasty lunch, or scoop it up with slices of avocado. Look for tuna that's packed in water, not oil, for the freshest-tasting tuna salad.

¼ cup extra-virgin olive oil

2 tablespoons lime juice

¼ teaspoon kosher salt

2 (5-ounce) cans tuna, drained

¼ cup diced celery

¼ cup sliced scallions, both white and green parts

¼ cup diced red bell pepper

1 tablespoon finely diced jalapeño pepper

2 tablespoons chopped fresh cilantro

MACRONUTRIENTS: 70% Fat, 25% Protein, 5% Carbs

1. Make the vinaigrette by whisking the olive oil, lime juice, and salt in a small bowl.

2. In a medium bowl, mix the tuna, celery, scallions, red bell pepper, and jalapeño pepper.

3. Add the vinaigrette and toss to coat, then top with the fresh cilantro. Serve and enjoy.

4. Refrigerate any leftovers in an airtight container for up to 3 to 4 days.

VARIATION: For a pretty—and tasty—presentation, serve this salad in half of an avocado. Just don't forget to add the nutritional information for the avocado to your meal.

PER SERVING: Calories: 181; Total fat: 14g; Saturated fat: 2g; Protein: 11g; Total carbohydrates: 3g; Fiber: 1g; Erythritol: 0g; Net carbs: 2g; Cholesterol: 20mg

BLT Salad

PREP TIME: 10 minutes | **SERVES 4**

Loaded with all the flavors of the classic sandwich but none of the carbs, this BLT salad is as hearty as it is delicious. I like using a variety of salad greens in this recipe, just to change it up. From spring mix to romaine and even kale, you can experiment to find all your favorite combinations.

8 slices bacon, chopped

2 tablespoons mayonnaise

2 tablespoons sour cream

¼ cup avocado oil

1 tablespoon lemon juice

Pinch kosher salt

Pinch freshly ground black pepper

6 cups bite-size lettuce, washed and dried

1 cup grape tomato halves

¼ cup sliced scallions, both white and green parts

MACRONUTRIENTS: 81% Fat, 12% Protein, 7% Carbs

1. In a medium skillet, fry the bacon over medium-high heat until it is cooked and crispy, about 6 minutes. Remove the bacon from the skillet with a slotted spoon and set it aside on a paper towel–lined plate.

2. Meanwhile, make the dressing. In a small bowl, whisk the mayonnaise and sour cream together. Pour in the avocado oil in a thin stream while whisking to create an emulsified dressing. Whisk in the lemon juice and season with the salt and pepper.

3. Evenly divide the lettuce among 4 shallow bowls.

4. Drizzle 2 tablespoons of dressing over each salad, and evenly divide the bacon, grape tomatoes, and scallions among them.

5. Refrigerate the undressed leftovers in the fridge for 2 to 3 days. The lettuce won't keep long once the dressing has been added.

VARIATION: Add even more protein to this salad with the addition of leftover cooked chicken, grilled shrimp, or even salmon.

PER SERVING: Calories: 311; Total fat: 28g; Saturated fat: 6g; Protein: 9g; Total carbohydrates: 6g; Fiber: 2g; Erythritol: 0g; Net carbs: 4g; Cholesterol: 29mg

GLUTEN-
FREE

NUT-
FREE

VEGE-
TARIAN

Egg Salad in Lettuce Cups

PREP TIME: 10 minutes | **COOK TIME:** 7 minutes | **SERVES 4**

Egg salad is a timeless classic for good reason: it's creamy, chunky, and delicious. And, when you make it this way, it's also a protein-rich keto-friendly meal. For lunch, dinner, or snacking, egg salad has well-rounded macros and is low in net carbs. Don't let the ingredient list shock you—this is the best egg salad you'll ever eat.

8 large eggs

2 tablespoons mayonnaise

2 tablespoons sour cream

2 tablespoons chopped scallions, both white and green parts

1 tablespoon lemon juice

1 tablespoon chopped fresh parsley

¼ teaspoon Italian seasoning

⅛ teaspoon garlic powder

⅛ teaspoon freshly ground black pepper

Romaine lettuce or butter lettuce leaves

MACRONUTRIENTS: 69% Fat, 27% Protein, 4% Carbs

1. Place the eggs in a medium pot and cover them with water. Bring the eggs to a boil over high heat and boil them for 7 minutes.

2. Take the eggs off the heat, cover the saucepan, and let it sit for 10 minutes. Then, cool the eggs in cold water and peel them.

3. Meanwhile, in a medium bowl, mix the mayonnaise, sour cream, scallions, lemon juice, parsley, Italian seasoning, garlic powder, and pepper.

4. Roughly chop the eggs and add them to the dressing, mixing well.

5. Place ¼ cup of egg salad into each lettuce cup and enjoy.

6. Refrigerate any leftover egg salad in an airtight container for up to 3 to 4 days. Leftover lettuce will keep in a zip-top plastic bag for up to 1 week.

VARIATION: Instead of sour cream, you can use all mayonnaise or use all sour cream for a tangier version of this delicious egg salad.

PER SERVING: Calories: 206; Total fat: 16g; Saturated fat: 5g; Protein: 13g; Total carbohydrates: 2g; Fiber: 0g; Erythritol: 0g; Net carbs: 2g; Cholesterol: 378mg

Meatball and Zucchini Noodle Soup

PREP TIME: 10 minutes | **COOK TIME:** 25 minutes | **SERVES 4**

This easy and tasty soup is packed with flavor, and by using zucchini noodles instead of pasta, we can keep the carbs in check. This is a versatile soup with meaty and tender meatballs. Feel free to embellish it with all your favorite vegetables. (See the tip for suggestions.)

FOR THE MEATBALLS

½ pound 80% lean ground beef

1 large egg

1 tablespoon Italian seasoning

½ teaspoon garlic salt

FOR THE SOUP

1 tablespoon salted butter

¼ cup diced yellow onion

2 garlic cloves, minced

4 cups low-sodium beef broth

1 (15-ounce) can diced tomatoes, undrained

1 tablespoon Italian seasoning

1 teaspoon kosher salt

¼ teaspoon freshly ground black pepper

2 cups zucchini noodles

¼ cup grated parmesan cheese, for garnish

MACRONUTRIENTS: 64% Fat, 24% Protein, 12% Carbs

TO MAKE THE MEATBALLS

1. In a medium bowl, mix the ground beef, egg, Italian seasoning, and garlic salt until combined. Create about 20 meatballs from the meat mixture and set them aside.

TO MAKE THE SOUP

2. Melt the butter in a large stockpot on medium heat and sauté the onion and garlic until the onion is translucent, about 5 minutes.

3. Add the meatballs to the pot, along with the beef broth, tomatoes, and Italian seasoning. Bring the mixture to a gentle simmer over low heat and simmer, uncovered, for 15 minutes or until the meatballs are no longer pink inside. Season with the salt and pepper.

4. Add the zucchini noodles to the soup and turn off the heat. The residual heat will cook the zucchini noodles.

5. Serve each serving of soup with a tablespoon of grated parmesan cheese on top.

6. Refrigerate the leftovers in an airtight container for up to 1 week. To reheat, warm the soup in a small saucepan on medium-low heat, or microwave it on high until it is heated through.

VARIATION: Add carrot, celery, broccoli, cauliflower, and even chopped kale or baby spinach to this hearty and robust soup.

PER SERVING: Calories: 247; Total fat: 18g; Saturated fat: 8g; Protein: 15g; Total carbohydrates: 8g; Fiber: 3g; Erythritol: 0g; Net carbs: 5g; Cholesterol: 100mg

Tabbouleh

PREP TIME: 10 minutes, plus 1 hour chilling time | **COOK TIME:** 10 minutes
SERVES 4

Tabbouleh is a classic Middle Eastern salad with a fresh and lively flavor. Traditional versions are made with bulgur, which is parboiled, dried, and cracked wheat kernels. Though this salad is usually high in carbs, we can make this delicious salad keto friendly with a few clever substitutes.

3 cups cauliflower rice

2 cups water

1 cup diced English cucumber

1 cup halved grape tomatoes

¼ cup chopped fresh parsley

¼ cup sliced scallions, both white and green parts

2 tablespoons lemon juice

¼ cup extra-virgin olive oil

¼ teaspoon kosher salt

⅛ teaspoon freshly ground black pepper

MACRONUTRIENTS: 79% Fat, 4% Protein, 17% Carbs

1. Combine the cauliflower rice and water in a medium saucepan, and bring to a boil over medium-high heat. Simmer for 1 minute, turn off the heat, and drain the cauliflower rice. Place it in the fridge to chill for 1 hour or overnight.

2. In a large bowl, mix the chilled cauliflower rice, cucumber, tomatoes, parsley, and scallions.

3. Measure the lemon juice into a small bowl. Whisk the olive oil in a thin stream into the lemon juice to create an emulsified vinaigrette. Season the dressing with the salt and pepper.

4. Before serving, toss the cauliflower rice mixture with the vinaigrette; serve chilled.

5. Refrigerate leftovers in an airtight container for up to 4 days.

PREP TIP: Cook the cauliflower rice ahead of time and chill it so the salad takes less time to prepare.

PER SERVING: Calories: 155; Total fat: 14g; Saturated fat: 2g; Protein: 2g; Total carbohydrates: 7g; Fiber: 3g; Erythritol: 0g; Net carbs: 4g; Cholesterol: 0mg

Unstuffed Pepper Soup

PREP TIME: 5 minutes | **COOK TIME:** 30 minutes | **SERVES 4**

Stuffed peppers are a delicious meal, but we can get all the flavors of this comfort food classic in soup form and keep it keto. This is a hearty soup, and *it freezes just fine, so make a double batch and keep extra portions on hand for a quick and easy meal another day.*

1 tablespoon avocado oil

½ pound 80% lean ground beef

¼ cup diced yellow onions

¼ cup diced celery

1 garlic clove, minced

4 cups low-sodium beef broth

1 (15-ounce) can diced tomatoes, undrained

1 tablespoon Italian seasoning

2 cups diced green bell peppers

2 cups cauliflower rice

½ teaspoon kosher salt

¼ teaspoon freshly ground black pepper

MACRONUTRIENTS: 63% Fat, 27% Protein, 10% Carbs

1. Heat the oil in a large, lidded stockpot over medium heat. Add the ground beef and brown it, breaking up the chunks until it is no longer pink, about 4 minutes.

2. Add the onions, celery, and garlic and sauté until the onion is soft and translucent, about 5 minutes.

3. Add the broth, diced tomatoes, and Italian seasoning to the beef mixture and increase the heat to high. Bring to a boil, reduce the heat to low, cover, and simmer for about 15 minutes.

4. Add the bell peppers and cauliflower rice and cook for an additional 2 minutes or until the vegetables are soft. Season with salt and pepper and serve.

5. Refrigerate any leftovers in an airtight container for up to 1 week, or freeze portions in airtight containers or zip-top plastic bags for up to 3 months.

   PREP TIP: Look for low- or no-sodium beef broth to control the sodium in this recipe.

PER SERVING: Calories: 519; Total fat: 37g; Saturated fat: 10g; Protein: 33g; Total carbohydrates: 14g; Fiber: 4g; Erythritol: 0g; Net carbs: 10g; Cholesterol: 165mg

Italian Vegetable Soup with Sausage

PREP TIME: 10 minutes | **COOK TIME:** 26 minutes | **SERVES 4**

This hearty, chunky soup is a keto favorite. Loaded with sausage, tender vegetables, and lots of flavor, it's like a hug in a bowl. Use your favorite Italian sausage—hot or mild—in this recipe; just be sure to read the ingredients label to look for hidden carbs. This recipe is quick to fix, and the leftovers will keep nicely for meals during the rest of the week.

1 tablespoon avocado oil

½ pound Italian sausage, casings removed

¼ cup diced yellow onion

¼ cup diced celery

½ cup sliced carrots

2 garlic cloves, minced

6 cups low-sodium chicken broth

2 cups chopped kale, stems removed

1 teaspoon kosher salt

¼ teaspoon freshly ground black pepper

MACRONUTRIENTS: 79% Fat, 15% Protein, 6% Carbs

1. Heat the oil in a large stockpot over medium-high heat and cook the Italian sausage, breaking it up into chunks, until it is no longer pink, about 6 minutes.

2. Add the diced onion, celery, carrots, and garlic to the sausage mixture. Reduce the heat to medium-low and cook for 5 minutes or until the onion is soft and translucent.

3. Add the chicken broth and kale, cover, and simmer for 15 minutes or until the kale is tender.

4. Season with salt and pepper and enjoy.

5. Refrigerate the leftovers in an airtight container for up to 1 week, or freeze portions in airtight containers or zip-top plastic bags for up to 3 months.

VARIATION: Don't care for kale? Use spinach instead, but add the spinach during the last 2 to 3 minutes of cook time.

PER SERVING: Calories: 245; Total fat: 21g; Saturated fat: 7g; Protein: 9g; Total carbohydrates: 4g; Fiber: 1g; Erythritol: 0g; Net carbs: 3g; Cholesterol: 43mg

Broccoli and Cheddar Soup

PREP TIME: 10 minutes | **COOK TIME:** 18 minutes | **SERVES 4**

Thick, creamy, and loaded with cheesy goodness, this soup is a comfort food classic that never goes out of style. With the keto twist, you can enjoy a hearty portion of this soul-warming soup guilt-free. Don't forget to save a bit of cheese to garnish the top of each bowl.

2 tablespoons salted butter

¼ cup diced yellow onion

¼ cup diced celery

2 garlic cloves, minced

4 cups broccoli florets

3 cups low-sodium chicken broth

4 ounces cream cheese

2 cups shredded Cheddar cheese

1 cup heavy cream

¼ teaspoon freshly ground black pepper

MACRONUTRIENTS: 81% Fat, 12% Protein, 7% Carbs

1. Melt the butter in a large stockpot over medium-high heat, and sauté the onion, celery, and garlic until the onion is soft and translucent, about 5 minutes.

2. Add the broccoli and chicken broth, increase the heat to high, cover, and bring to a boil. Reduce the heat to low and simmer for 10 minutes or until the broccoli is very soft.

3. Using an immersion blender or regular blender, puree the broccoli mixture until it is very smooth. If using a blender, be sure to put a towel over the top of the blender in case of spills.

4. Add the cream cheese and Cheddar to the soup and stir until both are melted. Place the soup on low heat, add the cream, and heat until the soup is hot. Season with the pepper (there should be enough salt in the soup from all the cheese), then serve.

5. Refrigerate any leftovers in an airtight container for up to 1 week.

VARIATION: For an extra indulgent soup, top with some chopped crispy bacon, thinly sliced scallions, or a dollop of sour cream.

PER SERVING: Calories: 607; Total fat: 55g; Saturated fat: 33g; Protein: 20g; Total carbohydrates: 11g; Fiber: 3g; Erythritol: 0g; Net carbs: 8g; Cholesterol: 180mg

Chicken Enchilada Soup

PREP TIME: 10 minutes | **COOK TIME:** 15 minutes | **SERVES 4**

Loaded with big and bold Southwestern flavors, this soup is creamy, chunky, and low in net carbs. Customize the spice level by adding more or less chipotle powder until it is as spicy as you like it.

2 tablespoons salted butter

1 cup frozen onion and bell pepper blend, roughly chopped

1 garlic clove, minced

2 tablespoons taco seasoning

½ teaspoon chipotle powder

1 (15-ounce) can diced fire-roasted tomatoes, undrained

2 cups low-sodium chicken broth

1 cup diced cooked chicken (store-bought rotisserie or leftovers)

½ cup heavy cream

½ teaspoon kosher salt

½ cup shredded Cheddar cheese

1. Melt the butter in a large stockpot over medium heat, and sauté the onion and bell pepper blend and garlic until the onion is soft and translucent, about 5 minutes.

2. Add the taco seasoning and chipotle powder and mix well.

3. Add the tomatoes and chicken broth, increase the heat to high, cover, and bring to a boil. Reduce the heat to low, and simmer, covered, for 10 minutes.

4. Add the chicken, cream, and salt and warm until hot but not boiling. Adjust the seasoning if necessary.

5. Garnish each bowl with 2 tablespoons of cheese and enjoy.

6. Refrigerate leftovers in an airtight container for up to 1 week.

PER SERVING: Calories: 310; Total fat: 23g; Saturated fat: 14g; Protein: 15g; Total carbohydrates: 11g; Fiber: 4g; Erythritol: 0g; Net carbs: 7g; Cholesterol: 97mg

MACRONUTRIENTS: 67% Fat, 20% Protein, 13% Carbs

SPICY VEGETABE STIR-FRY, PAGE 94

CHAPTER FIVE

Vegetables

MANY PEOPLE BELIEVE THAT A keto diet is a license to eat all the bacon and cheese they desire, but this isn't true. Vegetables are also important—not just because they're loaded with fiber, but for their nutritional value as well. In this chapter, I've included a variety of hearty and satisfying vegetable-centric meal-worthy dishes. From hearty stir-fries to casseroles, there's plenty to pick from if you're a vegetable lover. These recipes are inspired by the flavors of the globe, so try something different today.

Asparagus Frittata

PREP TIME: 10 minutes | **COOK TIME:** 25 minutes | **SERVES 4**

Similar to a hearty crustless quiche, frittata is a baked egg dish that can be loaded with many different flavors. In this version, I've packed the frittata with asparagus, cheese, and just enough onion to give it a bit more flavor. Feel free to mix and match with your favorite ingredients to customize this delicious one-pan meal.

1 pound asparagus spears

2 tablespoons salted butter

½ cup sliced scallions, white and green parts

6 large eggs

½ cup ricotta cheese

1 tablespoon fresh or dried chives

½ teaspoon kosher salt

¼ teaspoon freshly ground black pepper

1 cup shredded Jarlsberg cheese, divided

MACRONUTRIENTS: 67% Fat, 25% Protein, 7% Carbs

1. Preheat the oven to 350°F.

2. Prepare the asparagus by snapping off the tough stem ends and then cutting the asparagus into ½-inch-long pieces.

3. Melt the butter in a large oven-safe skillet over medium heat and add the asparagus. Cook for about 3 minutes or until the asparagus turns bright green and starts to soften.

4. Add the scallions and cook for 1 minute more.

5. Whisk the eggs in a small bowl. Add the ricotta cheese, chives, salt, and pepper and mix well. Fold in half of the Jarlsberg cheese.

6. Add the egg mixture to the skillet, stirring it around gently to evenly distribute the asparagus throughout the mixture.

7. Reduce the heat to low and cook until the bottom of the egg starts to set, 5 to 6 minutes. Then, transfer the skillet to the oven and cook for 10 to 12 minutes or until the egg is fully cooked.

8. Top the frittata with the remaining cheese, and brown the cheese under the broiler for 1 to 2 minutes.

9. Cut the frittata into wedges and serve.

10. Refrigerate any leftovers in an airtight container for up to 5 days.

SUBSTITUTION TIP: Instead of Jarlsberg, which tastes like a mild Swiss cheese, use Gouda or a pre-shredded Italian blend.

PER SERVING: Calories: 354; Total fat: 27g; Saturated fat: 14g; Protein: 22g; Total carbohydrates: 7g; Fiber: 3g; Erythritol: 0g; Net carbs: 4g Cholesterol: 339mg

Cabbage Skillet with Kielbasa

PREP TIME: 10 minutes | **COOK TIME:** 18 minutes | **SERVES 4**

Loaded with protein and fiber, this is the perfect keto dinner. It's hearty, has a great balance of macros, and is quick enough to turn even busy weeknights into feast nights. Look for kielbasa with no added starchy fillers to keep this recipe low in net carbs.

2 tablespoons salted butter

6 cups thinly sliced cabbage

¼ cup sliced yellow onion

2 garlic cloves, minced

1 pound kielbasa, halved lengthwise and cut into ¼-inch half-moons

2 tablespoons German- or Dijon-style mustard

2 tablespoons apple cider vinegar

½ teaspoon kosher salt

¼ teaspoon freshly ground black pepper

MACRONUTRIENTS: 67% Fat, 19% Protein, 14% Carbs

1. Heat the butter in a large skillet over medium heat until just melted. Add the cabbage and cook for about 5 minutes, then add the onion and garlic. Turn the heat down to medium-low and cook for an additional 10 minutes or until the cabbage has started to soften and cook down.

2. Add the kielbasa to the cabbage and stir well. Cook for an additional 3 to 4 minutes or until the kielbasa is hot.

3. In a small bowl, combine the mustard and vinegar, then add it to the cabbage mixture, mixing well to combine.

4. Season with the salt and pepper and serve.

5. Refrigerate any leftovers in an airtight container for up to 5 days.

SUBSTITUTION TIP: Instead of sausage, try this recipe with shrimp, chicken, or ground pork. Just make sure the proteins are thoroughly cooked before serving.

PER SERVING: Calories: 351; Total fat: 26g; Saturated fat: 11g; Protein: 17g; Total carbohydrates: 14g; Fiber: 3g; Erythritol: 0g; Net carbs: 11g; Cholesterol: 95mg

Portobello Kung Pao

PREP TIME: 10 minutes | **COOK TIME:** 10 minutes | **SERVES 4**

Inspired by the Chinese takeout classic, this vegetarian dish features meaty portobello mushrooms and a sweet, tangy, and spicy sauce. Serve it with plain cauliflower rice to soak up all the amazing sauce.

1 tablespoon avocado oil

6 portobello mushrooms, stems removed, black gills scraped out with a spoon, cut into ½-inch chunks

2 scallions, both white and green parts, cut into ½-inch pieces

1 green bell pepper, seeded and cut into ½-inch pieces

1 cup low-sodium chicken broth

5 tablespoons coconut aminos (or soy sauce)

1 tablespoon unseasoned rice wine vinegar

1 tablespoon brown sugar substitute

1 teaspoon sesame oil

¼ teaspoon xanthan gum (optional)

Kosher salt

Freshly ground black pepper

MACRONUTRIENTS: 50% Fat, 19% Protein, 31% Carbs

1. Heat the oil in a large skillet over medium-high heat. Add the diced mushrooms and cook for 2 to 3 minutes, stirring frequently.

2. Add the scallions and bell pepper and cook for 1 minute.

3. Meanwhile, make the sauce by mixing the chicken broth, coconut aminos, rice wine vinegar, brown sugar substitute, and sesame oil in a medium bowl.

4. When the peppers have softened, add the sauce to the skillet and turn the heat up enough so that it starts to boil. Simmer the sauce and vegetables for 2 minutes or until the sauce reduces and thickens a bit.

5. Thicken with the xanthan gum and season with salt and pepper. Enjoy.

INGREDIENT TIP: Xanthan gum is a powerful all-natural thickener, and a little goes a long way. Always start with a small amount of xanthan gum and whisk it into the liquids. Let it sit for a few minutes to thicken; ¼ teaspoon of xanthan gum is plenty for 1 cup of liquid.

PER SERVING: Calories: 97; Total fat: 5g; Saturated fat: 1g; Protein: 6g; Total carbohydrates: 8g; Fiber: 3g; Erythritol: 3g; Net carbs: 5g; Cholesterol: 0mg

Zucchini Cannelloni

PREP TIME: 10 minutes | **COOK TIME:** 24 minutes | **SERVES 4**

A tasty twist on an Italian classic, these cannelloni have all the flavor but none of the carbs of the pasta version. The filling is enlivened with spices and tender kale, but you can use spinach instead of kale. Perfect with a salad for lunch or dinner, this delicious meal is sure to become a favorite.

2 cups store-bought sugar-free marinara sauce

1 tablespoon salted butter

¼ cup diced yellow onion

1 garlic clove, minced

2 cups roughly chopped kale, stems removed

2 cups ricotta cheese

1 large egg

2 teaspoons Italian seasoning

1 cup shredded mozzarella cheese, divided

¼ teaspoon kosher salt

4 medium zucchini

MACRONUTRIENTS: 63% Fat, 26% Protein, 11% Carbs

1. Preheat the oven to 350°F.

2. Spread the marinara sauce evenly in the bottom of a 9-by-13-inch baking dish.

3. Melt the butter in a large skillet over medium heat. Add the onion and cook for 3 to 4 minutes or until it starts to soften. Add the garlic and the kale, mixing well. Reduce the heat to low and cook until the kale is wilted and soft, 5 to 6 minutes. Cool the kale and onion mixture.

4. In a medium bowl, mix the cooled kale and onion mixture with the ricotta, egg, and Italian seasoning. Add half of the shredded mozzarella cheese and mix well.

5. Cut off both ends of the zucchini. Using a vegetable peeler, create long, thin strips by peeling down the length of each zucchini. Stop when you get to the seed core.

6. On a flat work surface, lay 4 or 5 strips of zucchini in a line, slightly overlapping, with the shorter end toward you. Scoop 2 heaping tablespoons of filling onto the short end of the overlapping zucchini, then roll it up, jelly roll–style.

7. Nestle the filled and rolled zucchini cannelloni into the sauce in the baking dish. Repeat rolling and filling the zucchini cannelloni until your pan is full or there's no filling left.

8. Top the cannelloni with the remaining mozzarella cheese. Bake, uncovered, for 20 minutes or until the center is hot and bubbly.

9. Refrigerate any leftovers in an airtight container for up to 4 days.

SUBSTITUTION TIP: Instead of zucchini, try this recipe with eggplant or yellow summer squash.

PER SERVING: Calories: 374; Total fat: 27g; Saturated fat: 16g; Protein: 23g; Total carbohydrates: 11g; Fiber: 3g; Erythritol: 0g; Net carbs: 8g; Cholesterol: 139mg

Vegetable Biryani

PREP TIME: 10 minutes | **COOK TIME:** 10 minutes | **SERVES 4**

Layered with warm, exotic spices and plenty of flavor, this easy dish is so good, you won't even miss the meat. Bump up the protein with a spoonful of plain yogurt on top, or add a serving of grilled chicken or shrimp. With cooked-all-day flavor in a fraction of the time, this Indian-inspired dish is perfect for dinner tonight.

2 tablespoons salted butter or ghee

4 cups cauliflower rice

½ cup diced carrot

½ cup diced celery

¼ cup diced red onion

1 teaspoon garam masala

½ teaspoon ground turmeric

½ cup low-sodium chicken broth

1 cup diced zucchini

½ teaspoon kosher salt

Chopped fresh cilantro or mint (optional)

MACRONUTRIENTS: 56% Fat, 10% Protein, 34% Carbs

1. Melt the butter or ghee in a large skillet over medium heat. Add the cauliflower rice, carrot, celery, and red onion. Cook, stirring frequently, until the onion starts to soften, about 5 minutes.

2. Add the garam masala and turmeric to the skillet and mix well. Cook for 1 minute to release the flavor in the spices.

3. Add the chicken broth and zucchini, increase the heat to high, and cook for 3 to 4 minutes or until the liquid has mostly evaporated and the zucchini is soft.

4. Season with the salt, garnish with chopped cilantro or chopped mint (if using), and enjoy.

5. Refrigerate any leftovers in a sealed container for up to 4 days.

PER SERVING: Calories: 101; Total fat: 6g; Saturated fat: 4g; Protein: 3g; Total carbohydrates: 10g; Fiber: 3g; Erythritol: 0g; Net carbs: 7g; Cholesterol: 15mg

Bell Peppers Stuffed with Three Cheeses

PREP TIME: 15 minutes | **COOK TIME:** 15 minutes | **SERVES 4**

Stuffed bell peppers are usually loaded with rice, a no-no on a keto diet. But with this tasty version, you get all the amazing flavors in a keto-friendly package. They also reheat wonderfully.

1 tablespoon avocado oil

¼ cup diced yellow onion

2 cups ricotta cheese

½ cup parmesan cheese

1 large egg

1 tablespoon Italian seasoning

½ teaspoon kosher salt

¼ teaspoon freshly ground black pepper

4 large bell peppers, any color, cut in half vertically and seeded

1 cup store-bought sugar-free marinara sauce

2 cups shredded mozzarella cheese

MACRONUTRIENTS: 50% Fat, 33% Protein, 17% Carbs

1. Preheat the oven to 375°F.

2. Heat the oil in a medium skillet over medium heat and add the diced onion. Cook the onion until it is soft and translucent, about 5 minutes.

3. In a medium bowl, combine the onion, ricotta cheese, parmesan cheese, egg, Italian seasoning, salt, and pepper. Mix well.

4. Divide the marinara sauce among the peppers, placing 2 tablespoons in the bottom of each pepper.

5. Divide the ricotta mixture among the peppers, nestling spoonfuls into the peppers on top of the sauce. Top with the mozzarella cheese.

6. Place the filled peppers in a casserole dish large enough to hold them all in one layer. Bake for about 15 minutes or until hot and bubbly and the peppers have softened. Serve immediately.

7. Store any leftovers in an airtight container in the fridge for up to 4 days.

   VARIATION TIP: Add sliced mushrooms or diced zucchini to the filling before baking, and use an Italian cheese blend.

PER SERVING: Calories: 331; Total fat: 19g; Saturated fat: 10g; Protein: 26g; Total carbohydrates: 14g; Fiber: 4g; Erythritol: 0g; Net carbs: 10g; Cholesterol: 81mg

Broccoli and Cheese Zucchini Boats

PREP TIME: 10 minutes | **COOK TIME:** 15 minutes | **SERVES 4**

Zucchini boats are a fun and tasty way to enjoy a veggie-forward dish. Loaded with the rich and cheesy flavors of broccoli and Cheddar, these delicious boats can be served with your favorite proteins for a full and hearty meal or enjoyed alone as a lighter, but no less delicious, dish.

4 medium zucchini
½ cup heavy cream
4 ounces full-fat cream cheese
4 cups broccoli florets
1½ cups shredded sharp Cheddar cheese, divided

MACRONUTRIENTS: 77% Fat, 14% Protein, 9% Carbs

1. Preheat the oven to 375°F. Line a baking sheet with parchment paper.

2. Cut the ends off each zucchini, then halve them lengthwise. Use a soup spoon to scoop out the seeds from each zucchini half to create a boat. Be careful not to break through the sides or bottom of the zucchini. Discard the seeds.

3. In a small pot over low heat, heat the cream and cream cheese, whisking often, until the cream cheese melts.

4. Meanwhile, cut the broccoli florets into smaller chunks. They need to fit into the zucchini boats, so chop the broccoli small but don't pulverize it.

5. In a medium bowl, mix the chopped broccoli florets with the cream cheese mixture. Mix well, then mix in 1 cup of shredded sharp Cheddar cheese.

6. Place the zucchini boats on the prepared baking sheet. Fill each boat with about 1 cup of the broccoli mixture, mounding it up a bit.

7. Top the zucchini boats with the remaining Cheddar cheese. Bake for 10 to 12 minutes or until the broccoli mixture is bubbly and the zucchini softens.

8. Serve immediately. Refrigerate any leftovers in a sealed container for 3 to 4 days.

VARIATION TIP: Make this dish even heartier by adding some chopped cooked chicken, and mix and match with your favorite cheeses. Good choices are Gouda, pepper Jack, Swiss, and Colby-Jack.

PER SERVING: Calories: 414; Total fat: 36g; Saturated fat: 21g; Protein: 16g; Total carbohydrates: 10g; Fiber: 3g; Erythritol: 0g; Net carbs: 7g; Cholesterol: 115mg

Cauliflower and Broccoli Bake

PREP TIME: 10 minutes | **COOK TIME:** 30 minutes | **SERVES 4**

This is a hearty and satisfying casserole that does double duty both as a scrumptious side dish and a meatless main dish. This is a quick dish to pull together, so you can get everything prepped ahead of time and then pop it in the oven before eating. Fresh broccoli and cauliflower work best in this recipe, as frozen veggies tend to give off a fair bit of liquid and will dilute the sauce.

2 tablespoons salted butter

¼ cup diced yellow onion

1 garlic clove, minced

2 cups heavy cream

4 ounces cream cheese

½ teaspoon mustard powder

¼ teaspoon freshly ground black pepper

2 cups shredded sharp Cheddar cheese, divided

3 cups cauliflower florets

3 cups broccoli florets

MACRONUTRIENTS: 83% Fat, 10% Protein, 7% Carbs

1. Preheat the oven to 375°F.

2. In a large skillet, melt the butter over medium heat. Add the onion and cook until the onion begins to soften, about 5 minutes. Add the minced garlic and cook for 1 minute.

3. Add the cream and increase the heat to medium-high. Bring the cream to a simmer and then add the cream cheese. Whisk the sauce until the cream cheese has melted. Add the mustard powder and pepper and mix well.

4. Turn off the heat and add 1 cup of the shredded cheese. Mix well until the cheese is melted.

5. Transfer the sauce to a large bowl and add the cauliflower and broccoli florets. Toss to coat the vegetables with the sauce.

6. Pour the vegetables and any extra sauce into an 8-inch square casserole dish. Top with the remaining Cheddar cheese and bake for about 20 minutes or until the casserole is bubbling in the center and the vegetables are tender-crisp. Serve and enjoy.

7. Refrigerate leftovers in an airtight container for 3 to 4 days.

VARIATION TIP: Add some crunch to this dish by sprinkling 1 cup of pork panko (crushed pork rinds) over the top in the last 5 minutes of the baking time.

PER SERVING: Calories: 823; Total fat: 78g; Saturated fat: 47g; Protein: 22g; Total carbohydrates: 15g; Fiber: 4g; Erythritol: 0g; Net carbs: 11g; Cholesterol: 261mg

Zucchini Parmesan

PREP TIME: 15 minutes | **COOK TIME:** 30 minutes | **SERVES 4**

Zucchini parmesan is a riff on the Italian classic, chicken parmesan. This version is made keto friendly by omitting the breadcrumbs, but we can still get a crunchy and golden brown breading on the zucchini with a few tasty substitutes. Hearty and delicious, this recipe will cure your cravings for homemade Italian-style cuisine.

1½ cups sugar-free marinara sauce

4 medium zucchini

2 large eggs

1½ cups grated parmesan cheese, divided

1½ cups superfine almond flour

1 tablespoon Italian seasoning

2 tablespoons avocado oil

1 cup shredded mozzarella cheese

2 tablespoons chopped fresh basil

MACRONUTRIENTS: 65% Fat, 20% Protein, 15% Carbs

1. Preheat the oven to 375°F. Spread the marinara sauce in the bottom of an 8-inch square casserole dish. Set it aside.

2. Cut the ends off the zucchini and cut them lengthwise into ½-inch-thick planks. Set aside.

3. Whisk the eggs in a large, shallow dish. The dish should be large enough to hold a zucchini plank.

4. In another large, shallow dish, combine 1 cup of parmesan cheese with the almond flour and Italian seasoning and mix well.

5. Heat the oil in a large skillet over medium heat. Meanwhile, set up your dredging station.

6. When the oil is hot but not smoking, working one at a time, dip a zucchini plank into the egg mixture and then into the almond flour mixture, pressing the breading onto the zucchini to help it stick. Carefully lay the zucchini plank into the hot oil, and cook for about 2 minutes per side or until golden brown.

7. When browned, lay the zucchini plank in the casserole dish. Repeat.

8. When all the fried zucchini planks are in the casserole dish, overlapping if necessary, top the casserole with the mozzarella cheese and remaining parmesan.

9. Bake, uncovered, for about 20 minutes or until hot and bubbly and golden brown on top. Garnish with the chopped basil and serve immediately.

10. Refrigerate any leftovers in an airtight container for 2 to 3 days.

PER SERVING: Calories: 591; Total fat: 44g; Saturated fat: 13g; Protein: 31g; Total carbohydrates: 22g; Fiber: 7g; Erythritol: 0g; Net carbs: 15g; Cholesterol: 147mg

Broccoli Fried Rice

PREP TIME: 10 minutes | **COOK TIME:** 15 minutes | **SERVES 4**

You've heard of fried rice, and possibly even cauliflower fried rice, but did you know that you can make broccoli fried rice? This quick and tasty recipe is inspired by the Asian classic, and this keto vegetarian recipe is hearty enough to be a meal all on its own.

2 broccoli heads

2 tablespoons avocado oil

1 teaspoon sesame oil

¼ cup diced yellow onion

1 tablespoon peeled and minced fresh ginger

1 garlic clove, minced

1 large egg

2 tablespoons coconut aminos (or soy sauce)

Kosher salt

Freshly ground black pepper

¼ cup sliced scallions, both white and green parts

MACRONUTRIENTS: 81% Fat, 10% Protein, 9% Carbs

1. Trim the broccoli by cutting the crowns away from the stems. Use a vegetable peeler to peel the outside of the broccoli stems—it is fibrous and bitter. Cut the stems into 3 or 4 pieces, and chop the broccoli crowns into several smaller pieces.

2. Put the broccoli stems in a food processor and pulse until very roughly chopped. Add the florets and continue to pulse until the broccoli is finely chopped, but not pulverized. It should look like rice.

3. Heat the avocado and sesame oils in a large skillet over medium heat. Add the onion, ginger, and garlic. Cook, stirring frequently, until the onion is softened, about 5 minutes.

4. Add the broccoli rice to the skillet and continue to cook, stirring often, until the broccoli is bright green and softened, about 5 minutes.

5. Crack the egg into a small bowl and whisk well. Make a well in the center of the broccoli mixture and add the egg, using a spatula to scramble the egg in the middle of the skillet. Once the egg is cooked through, mix it with the rest of the broccoli mixture.

6. Add the coconut aminos (or soy sauce) and mix well. Season with salt and pepper and top with the scallions.

7. Refrigerate any leftovers in an airtight container for 3 to 4 days.

VARIATION TIP: Bump up the protein in this dish by browning half a pound of ground chicken or pork before adding the broccoli. Garnish with black and white sesame seeds for a pretty presentation.

PER SERVING: Calories: 102; Total fat: 9g; Saturated fat: 1g; Protein: 3g; Total carbohydrates: 2g; Fiber: 0g; Erythritol: 0g; Net carbs: 2g; Cholesterol: 47mg

Mushroom and Spinach Bake

PREP TIME: 10 minutes | **COOK TIME:** 25 minutes | **SERVES 4**

Mushroom fans will love this dish. It is loaded with two kinds of meaty mushrooms, lots of spinach, and a creamy sauce to tie it all together. This bake is satisfying and delicious but easy enough to pull together on a busy weeknight. Mix and match with all your favorite mushrooms, or use my suggestions.

Nonstick cooking spray

½ pound portobello mushroom caps

½ pound of cremini mushroom caps

2 tablespoons unsalted butter

¼ cup diced yellow onion

1 garlic clove, minced

1 pound baby spinach

1½ cups heavy cream

4 ounces cream cheese

½ teaspoon dried thyme

1½ cups shredded Jarlsberg cheese, divided

Kosher salt

Freshly ground black pepper

MACRONUTRIENTS: 82% Fat, 11% Protein, 7% Carbs

1. Preheat the oven to 350°F and spray the inside of an 8-inch square casserole dish with cooking spray.

2. Prepare the mushrooms by washing away any sediment. Scrape away the underside gills with a spoon. Dice the portobello mushrooms into ½-inch chunks, and cut the cremini mushrooms into ⅓-inch-thick slices.

3. Put the prepared mushrooms in a large skillet and add the butter. Cook the mushrooms over medium heat until they start to give off liquid, about 5 minutes.

4. Add the onion and garlic and continue cooking until the liquid is evaporated and the mushrooms begin to brown, 5 to 6 minutes.

5. Add the spinach, working in batches, if necessary, and use tongs to turn it over until the spinach has wilted, about 2 minutes. Let the spinach cook for 1 or 2 minutes to evaporate about half of the spinach liquid.

6. Reduce the heat to low and add the cream and cream cheese. Break up the cream cheese and cook until the cream cheese melts. Mix with the spinach and mushrooms.

7. Add the thyme and 1 cup of the Jarlsberg cheese. Mix well until the cheese melts. Adjust the seasoning, adding a pinch of salt if necessary and a few grinds of black pepper.

8. Transfer the mixture to the prepared casserole dish and top with the remaining cheese.

9. Bake for about 10 minutes, until the casserole is hot and bubbly and the cheese melts and browns. Serve immediately.

10. Refrigerate any leftovers in an airtight container for up to 4 days.

COOKING TIP: Before mushrooms can brown, they need to give off their excess liquid. Be patient. Once the liquid has evaporated, the mushrooms will begin to brown.

PER SERVING: Calories: 685; Total fat: 64g; Saturated fat: 38g; Protein: 21g; Total carbohydrates: 13g; Fiber: 4g; Erythritol: 0g; Net carbs: 9g; Cholesterol: 212mg

Baked Spanish Cauliflower Rice

PREP TIME: 10 minutes | **COOK TIME:** 25 minutes | **SERVES 4**

Big and bold tastes infuse this cheese-topped dish, making it a perfect pick on cool nights or whenever you need a flavor-packed meal. Substantial on its own or as a side dish for roasted or grilled meats, this veggie-forward dish is sure to please.

2 tablespoons avocado oil

¼ cup diced yellow onion

1 garlic clove, minced

½ cup low-sodium chicken broth

1 tablespoon tomato paste

1 tablespoon taco seasoning

4 cups cauliflower rice

½ green bell pepper, seeded and finely diced

1 cup shredded sharp Cheddar cheese

MACRONUTRIENTS: 68% Fat, 16% Protein, 16% Carbs

1. Preheat the oven to 375°F.

2. Heat the oil in a medium skillet over medium heat and add the onion. Sauté over medium heat until the onion starts to soften and becomes translucent, about 5 minutes. Add the garlic and cook for 1 minute or until fragrant.

3. Add the chicken broth, tomato paste, and taco seasoning to the skillet. Mix well to combine and bring it to a boil. Reduce the heat to low and simmer for 2 to 3 minutes.

4. Add the cauliflower rice and bell pepper and mix well.

5. Transfer the cauliflower rice mixture to an 8-inch square casserole dish. Sprinkle the cheese on top and bake for about 15 minutes or until hot and bubbly. Serve immediately.

6. Refrigerate leftovers in an airtight container for up to 4 days.

PER SERVING: Calories: 226; Total fat: 17g; Saturated fat: 6g; Protein: 10g; Total carbohydrates: 10g; Fiber: 3g; Erythritol: 0g; Net carbs: 7g; Cholesterol: 29mg

Vegetable Curry

PREP TIME: 10 minutes | **COOK TIME:** 20 minutes | **SERVES 4**

Mix and match your favorite keto-friendly vegetables to make this hearty curry. It's loaded with flavor, fiber, and the right amount of fat. This dish is even better the next day, so don't worry if you've got some leftovers.

1 tablespoon avocado oil

¼ cup diced yellow onion

2 garlic cloves, minced

1 tablespoon peeled and grated fresh ginger

1 cup low-sodium chicken broth

1 head cauliflower, cut into bite-size florets

2 cups green beans, cut into 1-inch pieces

1 red bell pepper, seeded and cut into strips

1½ tablespoons curry powder

1 (14-ounce) can full-fat coconut milk

Kosher salt

3 tablespoons chopped scallion, white and green parts, for garnishing (optional)

2 tablespoons chopped fresh cilantro, for garnishing (optional)

1. In a large pot or deep skillet with a fitted lid, heat the oil over medium heat. Add the onion and cook until it starts to soften and becomes translucent, about 5 minutes.

2. Add the garlic and ginger and cook for 1 minute or until aromatic.

3. Add the chicken broth, cauliflower, and green beans. Cover and bring to a boil. Simmer for 5 minutes or until the vegetables start to soften.

4. Remove the lid and simmer until the liquid is reduced by about half, 5 to 6 minutes.

5. Add the bell pepper and curry powder to the vegetables and mix well. Add the coconut milk and bring to a boil. Simmer, uncovered, for 2 to 3 minutes to thicken slightly.

6. Season with salt and serve garnished with sliced scallions (if using) and chopped cilantro (if using).

7. Refrigerate leftovers in an airtight container for up to 3 days.

SERVING TIP: The sauce in this dish is so good, you don't want to miss a drop. Serve with cauliflower rice to soak up this amazing sauce.

MACRONUTRIENTS: 74% Fat, 7% Protein, 19% Carbs

PER SERVING: Calories: 291; Total fat: 25g; Saturated fat: 19g; Protein: 6g; Total carbohydrates: 15g; Fiber: 5g; Erythritol: 0g; Net carbs: 10g; Cholesterol: 0mg

Spicy Vegetable Stir-Fry

PREP TIME: 10 minutes | **COOK TIME:** 15 minutes | **SERVES 4**

You can customize the heat in this spicy stir-fry by including more or less Sriracha; if you prefer a milder stir-fry, use half the recommended amount. There's baby corn in this recipe, and while corn isn't keto friendly, 1 cup of baby corn yields just 3 net carbs. Baby corn is also high in fiber and adds plenty of crunch.

2 tablespoons avocado oil

¼ cup sliced yellow onion

2 garlic cloves, minced

1 tablespoon peeled and grated fresh ginger

2 celery stalks, sliced

1 medium carrot, thinly sliced

1 cup canned baby corn, drained

1 green bell pepper, seeded and sliced

2 medium zucchini, cut into ⅓-inch-thick half-moons

2 tablespoons Sriracha

½ cup low-sodium chicken or vegetable broth

2 tablespoons coconut aminos or soy sauce

¼ teaspoon xanthan gum (optional)

¼ cup chopped peanuts, for garnishing (optional)

2 tablespoons chopped fresh cilantro, for garnishing (optional)

1 teaspoon sesame seeds, for garnishing (optional)

MACRONUTRIENTS: 50% Fat, 8% Protein, 42% Carbs

1. Heat the oil in a large skillet or wok over medium-high heat. Add the onion and cook for about 5 minutes or until it starts to soften.

2. Add the garlic and ginger and cook for 1 minute or until it is aromatic.

3. Reduce the heat to medium and add the celery and carrot. Cook for 2 to 3 minutes or until the vegetables start to soften.

4. Add the baby corn, green bell pepper, and zucchini and mix everything together. Cook for 3 to 4 minutes or until the vegetables are tender-crisp.

5. Add the Sriracha, chicken broth, and coconut aminos and mix well. Thicken with xanthan gum (if using) and serve.

6. Garnish this dish with a combination of peanuts, cilantro, and sesame seeds (if using).

7. Refrigerate leftovers in an airtight container for up to 4 days.

PER SERVING: Calories: 141; Total fat: 8g; Saturated fat: 1g; Protein: 4g; Total carbohydrates: 16g; Fiber: 4g; Erythritol: 0g; Net carbs: 12g; Cholesterol: 0mg

THAI-INSPIRED COCONUT-CURRY SHRIMP, PAGE 112

CHAPTER SIX

Fish and Shellfish

FOR THE MOST PART, FISH and seafood are low in carbs and perfect on a keto diet. In this chapter, I've created a variety of seafood and fish dishes packed with flavor. Love shrimp? Try the Thai-Inspired Coconut-Curry Shrimp, or go retro with a keto version of Tuna Casserole. You can customize many fish dishes by swapping the suggested fish with your favorite or with what's fresh at your grocery store's fish counter. From comfort food classics like Pan-Fried Cod and Slaw to saucy White Fish Ratatouille, you can jazz up your weekly meal routine with one of these tasty dishes.

Garlic Butter Shrimp and Vegetable Skillet

PREP TIME: 10 minutes | **COOK TIME:** 15 minutes | **SERVES 4**

Garlic, butter, and fresh dill add oodles of flavor to this quick and easy meal loaded with plump, sweet shrimp and lots of keto-friendly veggies. It's perfect for weeknight dinners, and if you pair it with cauliflower or broccoli rice, you can soak up all the delicious sauce. This recipe uses large shrimp, so look for bags marked 31/35, which indicates the number of shrimp per pound.

2 tablespoons salted butter, divided

1 pound large (31/35 count) shrimp, peeled and deveined

2 medium zucchini, halved lengthwise and cut into ⅓-inch-thick half-moons

1 red bell pepper, seeded and sliced thinly

1 garlic clove, minced

½ cup low-sodium chicken broth

1 tablespoon chopped fresh dill

¼ teaspoon kosher salt

Freshly ground black pepper

1. In a large skillet, heat 1 tablespoon of butter over medium heat until melted. Add the shrimp and cook for 2 to 3 minutes per side until they're pink, opaque, and starting to curl. Set them aside, leaving any liquid behind in the skillet.

2. Add the zucchini, bell pepper, and garlic to the skillet. Sauté for 3 to 4 minutes or until the zucchini starts to soften.

3. Add the chicken broth, dill, salt, and pepper. Simmer for 2 to 3 more minutes or until the veggies are tender and the sauce has reduced by about half.

4. Return the shrimp to the skillet and cook until heated through.

5. Serve immediately.

6. Refrigerate any leftovers in an airtight container for 2 to 3 days.

MACRONUTRIENTS: 40% Fat, 44% Protein, 16% Carbs

PER SERVING: Calories: 168; Total fat: 8g; Saturated fat: 4g; Protein: 18g; Total carbohydrates: 7g; Fiber: 2g; Erythritol: 0g; Net carbs: 5g; Cholesterol: 158mg

Cheesy Tuna Casserole

PREP TIME: 10 minutes | **COOK TIME:** 12 minutes | **SERVES 4**

Tuna casserole is one of those nostalgic recipes that never goes out of style. This version gets a keto makeover with zucchini noodles—or you can add well-drained and rinsed shirataki noodles instead.

1 tablespoon salted butter

1 garlic clove, minced

1 pound zucchini, spiralized

1 cup unsweetened almond milk

4 ounces cream cheese

1½ cup shredded sharp Cheddar cheese, divided

Freshly ground black pepper

2 (5-ounce) cans water-packed tuna

MACRONUTRIENTS: 67% Fat, 28% Protein, 5% Carbs

1. Preheat the oven to 375°F.

2. In a large skillet over medium heat, melt the butter and add the garlic. Cook the garlic for 1 minute or until it is fragrant, then add the zucchini noodles. Cook the noodles, turning often for about 2 minutes or until they start to soften. Remove the zucchini noodles from the skillet, discarding any liquid, and place them in the bottom of a 2-quart casserole dish.

3. Add the almond milk to the skillet and heat it over medium heat. Whisk in the cream cheese until it melts. Turn off the heat and stir in 1 cup of Cheddar cheese until melted. Add a few grinds of black pepper, to taste.

4. Drain the cans of tuna and add them to the sauce. Mix well to combine, then pour the tuna and sauce over the zucchini noodles.

5. Top with the remaining ½ cup of Cheddar cheese and bake for 10 to 12 minutes or until hot and bubbly. Serve immediately.

6. Refrigerate any leftovers in an airtight container for 2 to 3 days.

PER SERVING: Calories: 387; Total fat: 29g; Saturated fat: 16g; Protein: 27g; Total carbohydrates: 5g; Fiber: 1g; Erythritol: 0g; Net carbs: 4g; Cholesterol: 106mg

Sheet Pan Salmon and Asparagus

PREP TIME: 5 minutes | **COOK TIME:** 12 minutes | **SERVES 4**

Sheet pan recipes are the perfect one-pot meal. They are easy to clean up, and everything cooks at the same time, so there's little fuss. This dish combines the best of salmon and asparagus. You can skip the dill and use parsley, but don't skip fresh herbs altogether because they make this dish pop.

1 tablespoon salted butter

4 (6-ounce) salmon fillets

2 tablespoons Dijon mustard

2 garlic cloves, minced

1 tablespoon chopped fresh dill

1 teaspoon kosher salt, divided

1 pound asparagus, washed and trimmed

2 teaspoons lemon pepper

MACRONUTRIENTS: 42% Fat, 51% Protein, 7% Carbs

1. Preheat the oven to 350°F.

2. Place a medium sheet pan (a baking sheet with raised sides) in the oven for 1 or 2 minutes to warm it up.

3. Melt the butter on the warmed baking sheet, spreading it around to coat the middle of the sheet.

4. Place the salmon on the buttered baking sheet, leaving about 3 inches between each fillet.

5. In a small bowl, mix the Dijon mustard with the garlic and dill. Brush or spread this mixture evenly over the top of each fillet. Sprinkle the fish with about ½ teaspoon salt.

6. Lay the trimmed asparagus spears on the baking sheet between and around the salmon, but keep them close together. Don't spread them out too much or they might overcook.

7. Sprinkle the lemon pepper over the asparagus, then sprinkle with the remaining salt.

8. Bake for about 8 minutes, then remove the baking sheet from the oven and flip the asparagus over. Bake for 3 to 4 minutes longer, until the asparagus is tender-crisp and the salmon is flaky and cooked through.

SERVING TIP: For a pretty presentation and even more flavor, top each salmon fillet with 2 or 3 thin lemon slices before baking.

PER SERVING: Calories: 297; Total fat: 14g; Saturated fat: 4g; Protein: 37g; Total carbohydrates: 5g; Fiber: 3g; Erythritol: 0g; Net carbs: 2g; Cholesterol: 101mg

Shrimp and Cauliflower "Grits"

PREP TIME: 10 minutes | **COOK TIME:** 15 minutes | **SERVES 4**

Grits are loaded with carbs, making them a poor choice for anyone following a keto lifestyle. However, cauliflower can mimic the rich, creamy texture of grits, and with this recipe, you can enjoy a low-carb version of something that tastes remarkably similar to the real thing.

2 tablespoons salted butter, divided

4 cups cauliflower rice

1 cup unsweetened almond milk

¼ cup heavy cream

1 cup shredded white sharp Cheddar cheese

Kosher salt

1 pound large (31/35 count) shrimp, peeled and deveined

2 tablespoons Cajun seasoning

¼ cup sliced scallions, both white and green parts

Freshly ground black pepper

MACRONUTRIENTS: 61% Fat, 31% Protein, 8% Carbs

1. In a large skillet, melt 1 tablespoon of butter. Add the cauliflower rice and cook over medium heat until the cauliflower rice is tender and most of the water has evaporated, about 8 minutes.

2. Using a potato masher or immersion blender, puree the cauliflower rice until it is mashed but still chunky—granular but somewhat smooth, kind of like cooked grits.

3. Add the almond milk, cream, and sharp Cheddar. Heat over low heat and mix well. Add salt if necessary, but the cheese should be plenty salty.

4. Transfer the "grits" to a serving bowl and keep warm.

5. Wipe out the skillet with a paper towel and put it on the stove over medium heat. Melt the remaining butter in the skillet.

6. Meanwhile, toss the shrimp with the Cajun seasoning. Sauté the shrimp over medium heat for 2 to 3 minutes per side. They should be pink and opaque and starting to curl.

7. Top the cauliflower grits with the cooked shrimp, and drizzle the buttery sauce over top. Garnish with the sliced scallions and a few grinds of freshly ground black pepper.

VARIATION TIP: Like things spicy? Add ¼ teaspoon of cayenne or chipotle powder to the Cajun seasoning before seasoning the shrimp with it. That'll add a little bit more zing to this tasty recipe.

PER SERVING: Calories: 326; Total fat: 22g; Saturated fat: 13g; Protein: 25g; Total carbohydrates: 8g; Fiber: 2g; Erythritol: 0g; Net carbs: 6g; Cholesterol: 207mg

Roasted Cod and Peppers

PREP TIME: 10 minutes | **COOK TIME:** 12 minutes | **SERVES 4**

Light and flaky but still substantial, cod is a fabulous fish to enjoy while following a keto lifestyle. It pairs so well with many different ingredients. For this recipe, I've combined the fish with Italian flavors like pesto, peppers, and fresh tomatoes.

Nonstick cooking spray

1 red bell pepper, seeded and sliced

1 green bell pepper, seeded and sliced

1 cup halved grape tomatoes

½ cup sliced red onion

2 tablespoons extra-virgin olive oil

1 tablespoon Italian seasoning

4 (6-ounce) cod fillets, patted dry

½ teaspoon kosher salt

¼ teaspoon freshly ground black pepper

2 tablespoons store-bought pesto

MACRONUTRIENTS: 43% Fat, 47% Protein, 10% Carbs

1. Preheat the oven to 400°F. Spray an 8-inch square casserole dish with cooking spray.

2. Add the bell peppers, grape tomatoes, onion, olive oil, and Italian seasoning to the casserole dish, toss to combine, and spread the mixture in an even layer.

3. Nestle the fish on top of the vegetable mixture and season with the salt and pepper.

4. Bake for about 10 minutes, until the fish is flaky and opaque in the middle.

5. Remove the casserole dish from the oven and divide the pesto among the fillets, spreading it in an even layer on the fish.

6. Turn the oven to Broil and broil the fish for about 1 minute, until the pesto starts to bubble and lightly brown.

7. Serve immediately, spooning any liquid from the vegetables over the fish.

8. Refrigerate any leftovers for 2 to 3 days in an airtight container.

PER SERVING: Calories: 248; Total fat: 12g; Saturated fat: 2g; Protein: 28g; Total carbohydrates: 7g; Fiber: 2g; Erythritol: 0g; Net carbs: 5g; Cholesterol: 81mg

Pan-Fried Cod and Slaw

PREP TIME: 5 minutes | **COOK TIME:** 10 minutes | **SERVES 4**

Fish and chips get a keto makeover with this tasty dish. Golden-brown and delicious flaky fish pairs nicely with the creamy slaw. The best part is that this low-net-carb dish is an easy fix. Perfect for Fish Friday or whenever you're craving a tasty meal, this dish is a dinner winner.

Oil for shallow frying
4 (6-ounce) cod fillets
1 cup superfine almond flour
1 tablespoon Old Bay Seasoning
2 large eggs
½ cup mayonnaise
2 tablespoons powdered sugar substitute
1 tablespoon apple cider vinegar
Kosher salt
Freshly ground black pepper
1 (14-ounce) bag coleslaw mix

MACRONUTRIENTS: 62% Fat, 29% Protein, 9% Carbs

1. Heat ¼-inch of oil in a large skillet over medium heat.

2. Meanwhile, pat the fish dry with paper towels. In a shallow bowl, mix the almond flour with the Old Bay seasoning. In a second shallow bowl, whip the eggs until they're well mixed.

3. When the oil is hot but not smoking, dip the fillets one at a time into the egg and then into the almond flour mixture. Press the fillets into the almond flour lightly to help the coating stick.

4. Add the breaded fish to the oil and cook for 3 to 4 minutes or until golden brown. Carefully flip the fish over and cook for 3 minutes or until golden brown. Set them aside on a plate.

5. In a small bowl, mix the mayonnaise, sugar substitute, and vinegar. Season the dressing with salt and pepper, toss with the coleslaw mix, and serve alongside the crispy fish fillets.

6. Refrigerate any leftovers in an airtight container for 2 to 3 days.

SERVING TIP: Serve your fish with a wedge of lemon, and squeeze it over top before serving.

PER SERVING: Calories: 471; Total fat: 33g; Saturated fat: 5g; Protein: 33g; Total carbohydrates: 11g; Fiber: 4g; Erythritol: 6g; Net carbs: 7g; Cholesterol: 184mg

Shrimp in Cajun Cream Sauce with Zucchini Noodles

PREP TIME: 10 minutes | **COOK TIME:** 8 minutes | **SERVES 4**

This is a spin on a popular dish that features carb-heavy pasta, but in this version we've removed the carbs, using fun-to-eat zucchini noodles instead. This flavor-loaded dish is easy to master. Feel free to swap the zucchini noodles for shirataki noodles if you prefer.

2 cups spiralized zucchini

1 tablespoon salted butter

1 pound large (21/25 count) shrimp, peeled and deveined

1 tablespoon Cajun seasoning

1 cup heavy cream

2 teaspoons lemon juice

½ teaspoon kosher salt

Freshly ground black pepper

Diced tomatoes, for garnish

Chopped parsley, for garnish

Sliced scallions, for garnish

MACRONUTRIENTS: 72% Fat, 23% Protein, 5% Carbs

1. Bring a large pot of salted water to a boil over high heat. Add the zucchini noodles and cook for exactly 1 minute. Remove the zucchini noodles and shock them in cold water. Drain and set aside. The zucchini noodles should be bright green and tender-crisp.

2. Melt the butter in a large skillet over medium heat. While the butter is melting, toss the shrimp with the Cajun seasoning.

3. When the butter is hot but not browning, add the shrimp to the skillet. Cook for 2 to 3 minutes, then flip the shrimp and cook for 2 more minutes.

4. Turn the heat down to low and add the cream, stirring well to combine. Bring the cream to a simmer, then cook for about 2 minutes to reduce and thicken it a bit.

5. Add the lemon juice, salt, and pepper. Adjust the seasoning if necessary.

6. Return the zucchini noodles to the skillet and toss everything together. Cook on low heat for about 2 more minutes, just to heat the zucchini noodles through.

7. Serve topped with tomatoes, parsley, and scallions.

8. Refrigerate any leftovers for 2 to 3 days in an airtight container.

SUBSTITUTION TIP: To make this recipe dairy-free, use avocado oil in place of the butter, and use an equal measure of coconut milk instead of cream.

PER SERVING: Calories: 321; Total fat: 26g; Saturated fat: 16g; Protein: 17g; Total carbohydrates: 5g; Fiber: 1g; Erythritol: 0g; Net carbs: 4g; Cholesterol: 232mg

Baked Tilapia Piccata with Broccolini

PREP TIME: 10 minutes | **COOK TIME:** 15 minutes | **SERVES 4**

Tilapia is a light, flaky fish that's popular in the southern United States. If you can't find tilapia, other good choices include bass, sole, red snapper, or even catfish. The mild fish pairs perfectly with the lemony sauce, and the bright-green broccolini looks so pretty on the plate next to this stunning but oh so easy dish.

1 pound broccolini

2 tablespoons unsalted butter, divided

1 pound tilapia fillets

½ teaspoon kosher salt

Freshly ground black pepper

2 tablespoons diced shallots

1 garlic clove, minced

½ cup low-sodium chicken broth

2 tablespoons lemon juice

2 tablespoons capers (optional)

⅛ teaspoon xanthan gum (optional)

MACRONUTRIENTS: 35% Fat, 49% Protein, 16% Carbs

1. Bring a large pot of salted water to a boil over high heat. Trim the stem ends from the broccolini and drop them into the boiling water. Reduce the heat to medium-low and simmer the broccolini for 3 to 4 minutes or until it is fork-tender. Drain and cover to keep warm.

2. Meanwhile, melt 1 tablespoon of butter in a large skillet over medium-high heat. Season the fish fillets with the salt and pepper and fry them for 3 minutes, then flip them over and continue cooking until they're flaky and opaque, about 5 to 6 minutes total cooking time. Remove the fillets to a platter and cover loosely with aluminum foil to keep them warm.

3. To make the sauce, reduce the heat to medium and melt the remaining tablespoon of butter. Add the shallots and garlic and sauté for 2 to 3 minutes, until fragrant.

4. Add the chicken broth and bring the mixture to a simmer. Simmer for 2 minutes to reduce slightly.

5. Add the lemon juice and capers. Adjust the seasoning, if necessary. Thicken with the xanthan gum (if using) by whisking it in and letting the sauce rest for 2 minutes.

6. Drizzle the sauce over the fish and serve with the broccolini on the side. Garnish with some chopped fresh parsley for a pop of color and freshness.

SUBSTITUTION TIP: Capers are unopened flower buds that grow on bushes in the Mediterranean. They are brined or pickled and have a lovely lemony-herbal flavor that works so well in this dish. If you can't find them or don't care for them feel free to leave them out. Diced red bell pepper would be a lovely and colorful substitute.

PER SERVING: Calories: 210; Total fat: 8g; Saturated fat: 4g; Protein: 27g; Total carbohydrates: 10g; Fiber: 3g; Erythritol: 0g; Net carbs: 7g; Cholesterol: 72mg

Fish Cakes with Garlic Sauce

PREP TIME: 10 minutes | **COOK TIME:** 20 minutes | **SERVES 4**

These fish cakes are a nostalgic dish that's so tasty when paired with the garlic sauce. They are crispy on the outside and loaded with plenty of flaky fish, herbs, and seasonings inside. Serve this dish with a bright-green vegetable or side salad for a filling and satisfying meal.

1½ pounds white fish, such as haddock, cod, or pollack

2 cups cauliflower rice

2 large eggs

1 cup superfine almond flour

¼ cup oat fiber

2 tablespoons chopped fresh parsley

1 scallion, both white and green parts, sliced

½ teaspoon kosher salt

¼ teaspoon freshly ground black pepper

Oil for frying

½ cup mayonnaise

½ teaspoon garlic powder

MACRONUTRIENTS: 64% Fat, 28% Protein, 8% Carbs

1. Preheat the oven to 375°F and bake the fish on a parchment paper–lined baking sheet until it is flaky and opaque, 12 to 15 minutes. Let the fish cool slightly. This step can be done the day before.

2. In a large skillet over medium heat, cook the cauliflower rice in ½ cup of water until the water has evaporated and the cauliflower is tender. Drain any excess water, and transfer the cauliflower to a large bowl.

3. Add the fish to the cauliflower, breaking it up into flakes. Add the eggs, almond flour, oat fiber, parsley, scallion, salt, and pepper and mix well with a large spoon.

4. Form the fish mixture into about 8 patties, pressing them gently to keep the mixture together.

5. Heat about ½ inch of oil in a large skillet over medium-high heat until it is hot but not smoking. Gently lay the fish cakes in the oil, working in batches if necessary, and fry them until they're golden brown, about 4 minutes. Flip them over and fry them on the other side for 4 minutes. Turn down the heat if they're browning too quickly.

6. In a small bowl, mix the mayonnaise with the garlic powder. Serve the sauce with the piping hot fish cakes.

7. Refrigerate any leftovers in an airtight container for 2 to 3 days.

PER SERVING: Calories: 548; Total fat: 40g; Saturated fat: 5g; Protein: 38g; Total carbohydrates: 13g; Fiber: 5g; Erythritol: 0g; Net carbs: 8g; Cholesterol: 196mg

Thai-Inspired Coconut-Curry Shrimp

PREP TIME: 10 minutes | **COOK TIME:** 10 minutes | **SERVES 4**

Coconut and curry pair together so nicely in this light and flavorful dish, and the succulent, sweet shrimp are a meaty addition. Feel free to jazz up this dish with more vegetables. Keto-friendly veggies that pair with this dish are bok choy, bean sprouts, and cabbage.

2 tablespoons avocado oil

½ cup sliced red onion

1 (1-inch) piece ginger, minced

1 garlic clove, minced

1½ pounds large (21/25 count) shrimp, peeled and deveined

1 red bell pepper, seeded and sliced

1 (14-ounce) can full-fat coconut milk

1 teaspoon Thai red curry paste

1 tablespoon lime juice

Kosher salt

Freshly ground black pepper

⅛ teaspoon xanthan gum (optional)

Cilantro, chopped peanuts, chopped Thai basil, or sliced scallions to garnish

1. Heat the oil in a large skillet over medium heat.

2. When the oil is hot but not smoking, add the onion, ginger, and garlic and sauté for 2 to 3 minutes or until the onions start to soften.

3. Add the shrimp and bell pepper to the skillet and cook for 2 to 3 minutes, then flip the shrimp over. Continue cooking for an additional 2 minutes or until the shrimp are pink and opaque and starting to curl up.

4. Add the coconut milk and red curry paste. Mix well to combine. Add the lime juice and season with salt and pepper. Thicken with the xanthan gum if desired. Garnish with your favorite toppings and serve.

5. Refrigerate any leftovers in an airtight container for 2 to 3 days.

PER SERVING: Calories: 397; Total fat: 30g; Saturated fat: 20g; Protein: 26g; Total carbohydrates: 8g; Fiber: 1g; Erythritol: 0g; Net carbs: 7g; Cholesterol: 214mg

MACRONUTRIENTS: 64% Fat, 27% Protein, 9% Carbs

Shrimp and Sausage Jambalaya

PREP TIME: 10 minutes | **COOK TIME:** 25 minutes | **SERVES 4**

This classic New Orleans–inspired dish is big and bold and goes keto with a few substitutions to lighten the carb count. There's no lack of flavor in this dish, and it's hearty enough that you don't need anything else with it, except for maybe a small salad.

2 tablespoons avocado oil

½ cup diced yellow onion

½ cup diced celery

½ cup finely chopped green bell pepper

1 pound andouille sausage, cut into ½-inch-thick rounds

1 (28-ounce) can diced tomatoes

1 tablespoon Cajun seasoning

1 pound large (21/25 count) shrimp, peeled and deveined

2 cups cauliflower rice

Kosher salt

Freshly ground black pepper

MACRONUTRIENTS: 67% Fat, 24% Protein, 9% Carbs

1. Heat the oil in a large skillet over medium heat.

2. When the oil is hot but not smoking, add the onion, celery, and bell pepper and cook for 3 to 4 minutes or until the onion starts to soften.

3. Add the andouille sausage and cook for 3 to 4 minutes, until the onion is soft but not brown and the oils start to come out of the sausage.

4. Add the diced tomatoes and Cajun seasoning to the skillet and mix well to combine. Reduce the heat to low, cover, and simmer for about 10 minutes, stirring once or twice.

5. Add the shrimp and cauliflower rice to the skillet and mix well. Bring the mixture back to a simmer and cook for 5 to 6 minutes, until the shrimp are cooked and the cauliflower is tender. Season with salt and pepper and serve.

6. Refrigerate any leftovers in an airtight container for 2 to 3 days.

SERVING TIP: Garnish this pretty dish with chopped fresh parsley, a squeeze of lemon, and sliced scallions.

PER SERVING: Calories: 594; Total fat: 44g; Saturated fat: 14g; Protein: 35g; Total carbohydrates: 14g; Fiber: 6g; Erythritol: 0g; Net carbs: 8g; Cholesterol: 229mg

White Fish Ratatouille

PREP TIME: 10 minutes | **COOK TIME:** 20 minutes | **SERVES 4**

Inspired by the famous French dish, this ratatouille takes the best of the original and jazzes it up with flaky fish. The combination of flavors is remarkable, and it can be made with cod, pollack, haddock, catfish, or any other firm white fish.

2 tablespoons avocado oil

1 cup diced eggplant

½ cup diced yellow onion

1 garlic clove, minced

1 medium zucchini, diced

1 medium yellow summer squash, diced

1 (14½-ounce) can diced tomatoes, undrained

1 teaspoon fines herbes seasoning blend

1½ pounds white fish fillets

½ teaspoon kosher salt

MACRONUTRIENTS: 32% Fat, 53% Protein, 15% Carbs

1. Heat the oil in a large skillet over medium heat.

2. When the oil is hot but not smoking, add the diced eggplant and cook over medium heat, stirring often, for 2 minutes.

3. Add the onion and garlic and cook for 4 to 5 minutes or until the onion starts to soften.

4. Add the diced zucchini, summer squash, and tomatoes and mix well. Cook over medium heat for 3 to 4 minutes or until the liquid has reduced by about a third.

5. Add the fines herbs to the skillet and mix well.

6. Make 4 wells in the tomato mixture, and nestle a fish fillet in each well. Cover the skillet and cook over medium-low heat for about 10 minutes or until the fish flakes easily and is opaque in the middle.

7. Season with the salt and serve.

8. Refrigerate leftovers in an airtight container for up to 4 days.

SUBSTITUTION TIP: No fines herbs? Substitute with ¼ teaspoon dried thyme, ¼ teaspoon dried rosemary, ¼ teaspoon dried chives, and ¼ teaspoon dried parsley.

PER SERVING: Calories: 235; Total fat: 8g; Saturated fat: 1g; Protein: 30g; Total carbohydrates: 10g; Fiber: 4g; Erythritol: 0g; Net carbs: 6g; Cholesterol: 92mg

CHICKEN PARMESAN, PAGE 122

CHAPTER SEVEN

Poultry

CHICKEN IS THE MOST COMMONLY consumed meat on the planet for good reason. It is affordable, widely available, and versatile. I've included some of my most flavorful poultry dishes for you to try. Some dishes are lighter, and others are veritable feasts. But they're all easy to make and are crafted from easily found ingredients. Whether you love spending time in the kitchen or want a quick meal on the go, there's something delicious to tempt you in this chapter.

Chicken, Broccoli, and Cauliflower Teriyaki Skillet

PREP TIME: 10 minutes | **COOK TIME:** 10 minutes | **SERVES 4**

Loaded with broccoli and a well-balanced sauce that's not too sweet, this skillet meal is hearty and satisfying. Customize it with all your favorite veggies, and serve it over shirataki or cauliflower rice to soak up all that delicious sauce. Quick-cooking chicken tenders add to the appeal of this dish, making it a great pick for busy evenings.

1 tablespoon avocado oil

1 pound chicken tenders, cut into bite-size pieces

¼ cup coconut aminos or soy sauce

2 tablespoons brown sugar substitute

2 teaspoons sesame oil

1 teaspoon peeled and grated fresh ginger

2 garlic cloves, finely minced

⅛ teaspoon xanthan powder (optional)

1 (16-ounce) bag frozen chopped cauliflower and broccoli

1. Heat the oil in a large skillet over medium heat.

2. When the oil is hot but not smoking, add the chicken and cook for 4 to 5 minutes, stirring often, until the chicken is no longer pink inside.

3. Meanwhile, make the sauce. In a small bowl, blend the coconut aminos, brown sugar substitute, sesame oil, ginger, and garlic. Thicken with the xanthan gum, if desired, by whisking it in and letting the sauce stand for a few minutes.

4. Add the frozen vegetables to the chicken and cook for 2 minutes, then add the teriyaki sauce.

5. Reduce the heat to low and cook for 2 minutes or until the vegetables are heated through. Serve hot.

6. Refrigerate leftovers in an airtight container for up to 4 days.

MACRONUTRIENTS: 33% Fat, 58% Protein, 9% Carbs

PER SERVING: Calories: 212; Total fat: 8g; Saturated fat: 1g; Protein: 30g; Total carbohydrates: 5g; Fiber: 3g; Erythritol: 6g; Net carbs: 2g; Cholesterol: 66mg

Chicken Broccoli Alfredo

PREP TIME: 10 minutes | **COOK TIME:** 15 minutes | **SERVES 4**

Loaded with tender strips of chicken, this is a creamy, garlicky, cheesy dish everyone can enjoy. And it's easy to make, too! Frozen broccoli cuts down on prep time, and the keto-friendly sauce comes together in just a few minutes.

1 tablespoon avocado oil

1 pound boneless, skinless chicken breast, cut into ½-inch-thick slices

½ teaspoon kosher salt

¼ teaspoon freshly ground black pepper

1 tablespoon salted butter

1 garlic clove, minced

1 (16-ounce) bag chopped frozen broccoli

2 cups heavy cream

¼ cup freshly grated parmesan cheese, plus more for serving

MACRONUTRIENTS: 74% Fat, 20% Protein, 6% Carbs

1. Heat the oil in a large skillet over medium heat.

2. Season the chicken with the salt and pepper. When the oil is hot but not smoking, add the chicken. Cook for 6 to 8 minutes or until it is fully cooked and no longer pink inside.

3. Add the butter and garlic and cook for 1 minute or until the garlic is fragrant.

4. Add the broccoli and cook for 2 minutes to thaw the broccoli.

5. Add the cream and bring the mixture to a simmer. Simmer for 3 minutes to thicken slightly, then turn off the heat.

6. Add the parmesan cheese and stir well. Serve with extra parmesan on top, plus a few grinds of freshly ground black pepper.

7. Refrigerate leftovers in an airtight container for up to 5 days.

PER SERVING: Calories: 663; Total fat: 55g; Saturated fat: 31g; Protein: 33g; Total carbohydrates: 11g; Fiber: 3g; Erythritol: 0g; Net carbs: 8g; Cholesterol: 259mg

Turkey Enchilada Bowl

PREP TIME: 5 minutes | **COOK TIME:** 15 minutes | **SERVES 4**

This fun dish is packed with big and bold Southwestern flavors. I created this recipe thinking of the delicious food I enjoyed while living for more than 20 years in Texas. Grab your chipotle powder and your spices because this dish is bursting with flavor.

1 tablespoon avocado oil

1 pound lean ground turkey

¼ cup diced yellow onion

8 ounces canned tomato puree

½ cup low-sodium chicken broth

1 tablespoon chili powder

1 teaspoon ground cumin

½ teaspoon chipotle powder

½ teaspoon garlic powder

Kosher salt

Freshly ground black pepper

Garnishes: Cheese, chopped cilantro, diced avocado, sliced jalapeños, or sour cream.

MACRONUTRIENTS: 49% Fat, 40% Protein, 11% Carbs

1. In a large skillet over medium heat, heat the oil. Add the ground turkey and cook for 3 to 4 minutes, until it starts to brown.

2. Add the onion and cook for an additional 5 to 6 minutes, until the onion is soft and the ground turkey is no longer pink.

3. Add the canned tomato puree, chicken broth, chili powder, cumin, chipotle powder, and garlic powder. Mix well and bring to a simmer over low heat. Simmer for 3 to 4 minutes, then season with salt and pepper.

4. Serve topped with your favorite garnishes.

5. Refrigerate leftovers in an airtight container for up to 5 days.

PER SERVING: Calories: 233; Total fat: 13g; Saturated fat: 3g; Protein: 24g; Total carbohydrates: 7g; Fiber: 2g; Erythritol: 0g; Net carbs: 5g; Cholesterol: 78mg

Thai-Inspired Lettuce Wraps

PREP TIME: 5 minutes | **COOK TIME:** 10 minutes | **SERVES 4**

These delicious wraps make a fabulous dinner. The crunchy peanut and crisp bean sprout topping is satisfying. The subtle peanut flavor and loads of ginger combine nicely to give the ground turkey a lovely flavor.

1 tablespoon avocado oil

2 tablespoons peeled and grated fresh ginger

1 garlic clove, minced

1 pound lean ground turkey

¼ cup low-sodium chicken broth

1 tablespoon sugar-free fish sauce (optional but highly suggested)

2 tablespoons lime juice

1 teaspoon brown sugar substitute

1 tablespoon natural peanut butter

8 large lettuce leaves, romaine, butter lettuce or iceberg

Garnishes: Cilantro, bean sprouts, sliced scallions, sliced jalapeños, or sliced bird's eye chile.

MACRONUTRIENTS: 57% Fat, 38% Protein, 5% Carbs

1. Heat the oil in a large skillet over medium heat. Add the ginger and garlic and cook for 1 to 2 minutes, until fragrant; be careful not to let them burn.

2. Add the ground turkey, and use a spatula to break it up and mix it with the ginger and garlic. Cook for 5 to 6 minutes or until the turkey is no longer pink and much of the liquid has evaporated.

3. Meanwhile, in a small bowl, mix the chicken broth, fish sauce, lime juice, and peanut butter. Add this mixture to the ground turkey, and cook for 2 to 3 minutes or until most of the liquid has evaporated.

4. Add ⅓ cup of the turkey mixture to a lettuce cup, top it with your favorite garnishes, and enjoy.

5. Refrigerate leftovers in an airtight container for up to 5 days.

INGREDIENT TIP: Fish sauce has a very strong flavor right out of the bottle, but it adds so much umami to a dish that I recommend using it, unless you have a fish or shellfish allergy. There are sugar-free brands available; just be sure to read the ingredient labels.

PER SERVING: Calories: 237; Total fat: 15g; Saturated fat: 3g; Protein: 23g; Total carbohydrates: 3g; Fiber: 1g; Erythritol: 1g; Net carbs: 2g; Cholesterol: 84mg

Chicken Parmesan

PREP TIME: 10 minutes | **COOK TIME:** 15 minutes | **SERVES 4**

Fresh basil and fresh tomatoes are the key to this dish's success, and with so much flavor, you won't even miss the pasta. If you do have to have your noodles, serve the chicken with a side of zucchini noodles shirataki noodles. This saucy and cheesy dish is a comfort food classic.

1½ cups superfine almond flour

1 cup grated parmesan cheese, divided

2 large eggs

1 pound boneless, skinless chicken breasts, cut in half horizontally

¼ cup avocado oil, divided

1½ cups sugar-free marinara sauce

1 cup cherry tomato halves

1 tablespoon Italian seasoning

2 cups shredded mozzarella

Fresh basil to garnish

MACRONUTRIENTS: 60% Fat, 33% Protein, 7% Carbs

1. Preheat the oven to 400°F.

2. In a shallow bowl, combine the almond flour and ½ cup parmesan cheese. In a second shallow bowl, whisk the eggs.

3. Working with one piece of chicken at a time, dredge the chicken breast first into the egg and then into the almond flour–parmesan mixture. Set the breaded piece of chicken aside and repeat.

4. Heat 2 tablespoons of avocado oil in a large skillet over medium heat. When the oil is hot, carefully lay 2 of the chicken pieces in the skillet. Fry for 3 to 4 minutes per side, until the chicken is golden brown. Set the cooked chicken breasts aside and repeat, adding more oil if necessary.

5. Meanwhile, in a medium saucepan over medium-low heat, simmer the marinara sauce with the cherry tomatoes and Italian seasoning. Stir the sauce often so it doesn't burn on the bottom.

6. Spread the marinara sauce in the bottom of an 8-inch square casserole dish, then lay the fried chicken breasts on the sauce, overlapping them slightly, if necessary.

7. Top the chicken with the mozzarella and bake, uncovered, for 5 to 6 minutes or until the cheese has melted and is starting to bubble.

8. Serve with fresh basil and enjoy.

SUBSTITUTION TIP: Instead of almond flour, try breading the chicken with pork panko (finely ground pork rinds). They have a neutral flavor and add plenty of crunch to this chicken dish.

PER SERVING: Calories: 622; Total fat: 43g; Saturated fat: 13g; Protein: 49g; Total carbohydrates: 11g; Fiber: 4g; Erythritol: 0g; Net carbs: 7g; Cholesterol: 213mg

Thai-Inspired Basil Chicken

PREP TIME: 10 minutes | **COOK TIME:** 15 minutes | **SERVES 4**

This is a pretty dish that's loaded with colorful vegetables and plenty of flavor. It's got coconut milk–based sauce, so it's a good dairy-free option. And, since it is low in net carbs, you can make it when you don't have a lot of free time.

1 pound boneless, skinless chicken breasts, cut into 1-inch chunks

Kosher salt

Freshly ground black pepper

2 tablespoons avocado oil

2 cups green beans, blanched (see tip)

1 red bell pepper, seeded and cut into strips

1 garlic clove, minced

1 (15-ounce) can coconut milk

2 tablespoons lime juice

1 tablespoon brown sugar substitute

1 tablespoon coconut aminos or soy sauce

10 fresh basil leaves, chopped

⅛ teaspoon xanthan gum (optional)

¼ cup chopped roasted peanuts, for garnishing (optional)

½ jalapeño pepper, seeded and thinly sliced, for garnishing (optional)

Lime wedges, for garnishing (optional)

MACRONUTRIENTS: 63% Fat, 28% Protein, 9% Carbs

1. Season the chicken with salt and pepper.

2. Heat the oil in a wok or large skillet until it is hot but not smoking. Add the chicken and stir-fry over medium-high heat for 6 to 8 minutes, stirring often, until cooked and no longer pink inside.

3. Add the green beans, red bell pepper, and garlic and cook for 2 minutes.

4. Add the coconut milk, lime juice, brown sugar substitute, and coconut aminos; cook for 2 minutes to blend all the flavors together. Stir in the basil and turn off the heat.

5. Thicken with xanthan gum (if using).

6. Garnish with peanuts, jalapeño, or a wedge of lime (if using).

> **COOKING TIP:** Blanching the beans precooks them so they can work in quick stir-fries like this one. To blanch beans, bring a pot of salted water to a rolling boil. Add the beans and bring the water back to a simmer for 1 minute, then drain the beans and shock them in ice water to stop them from cooking.

PER SERVING: Calories: 424; Total fat: 32g; Saturated fat: 21g; Protein: 29g; Total carbohydrates: 9g; Fiber: 2g; Erythritol: 3g; Net carbs: 7g; Cholesterol: 65mg

Garlic Butter Chicken with Cauliflower Rice

PREP TIME: 10 minutes | **COOK TIME:** 15 minutes | **SERVES 4**

Tender chunks of chicken are enveloped in a garlic butter that's simply too good to resist. A fresh pop of color from the herbs adds plenty of flavor and eye appeal, making this dish a stunning—and remarkably easy—meal. Serve it with cauliflower rice to soak up all that amazing sauce.

4 tablespoons cold salted butter, divided

1 pound boneless, skinless chicken breast, cut into 1-inch cubes

1 teaspoon kosher salt, divided

¼ teaspoon freshly ground black pepper

2 garlic cloves, minced

½ cup low-sodium chicken broth

3 cups cauliflower rice

¼ cup water

2 tablespoons chopped fresh parsley

¼ teaspoon paprika

MACRONUTRIENTS: 48% Fat, 45% Protein, 7% Carbs

1. In a large skillet over medium heat, melt 2 tablespoons butter.

2. Season the chicken with ½ teaspoon of salt and the pepper. Add the chicken to the skillet and cook over medium heat for 3 to 4 minutes, then flip the chicken and cook for an additional 3 to 4 minutes or until cooked through. Remove the chicken from the skillet and set it aside on a plate.

3. Add the garlic to the skillet and cook for 1 minute or until aromatic. Add the chicken broth and simmer until reduced by half, about 4 minutes.

4. Meanwhile, put the cauliflower rice, water, and remaining ½ teaspoon salt in a microwave-safe bowl, cover with plastic wrap, and cook on high for about 3 minutes or until the cauliflower is tender. Stir it and drain.

5. Turn the heat off under the skillet and add the remaining 2 tablespoons of cold butter to the skillet, swirling to slowly melt the butter. This will thicken the sauce somewhat.

6. Return the chicken to the skillet along with any juices from the plate, and top with the parsley and paprika.

7. Serve the chicken with a generous spoonful of sauce on a bed of cauliflower rice.

8. Refrigerate in an airtight container for up to 5 days.

SUBSTITUTION TIP: Turkey is also delicious when cooked like this; look for boneless turkey breast.

PER SERVING: Calories: 254; Total fat: 14g; Saturated fat: 8g; Protein: 28g; Total carbohydrates: 5g; Fiber: 2g; Erythritol: 0g; Net carbs: 3g; Cholesterol: 95mg

Chicken Paprikash with Mashed Cauliflower

PREP TIME: 10 minutes | **COOK TIME:** 20 minutes | **SERVES 4**

Inspired by the Hungarian classic, this version has been modified so you don't have to cook all day long. Serve this saucy and delicious dish with mashed cauliflower. If you'd like, add a dollop of sour cream to go on top.

FOR THE CHICKEN PAPRIKASH

1 pound boneless, skinless chicken thighs, cut into strips

½ teaspoon kosher salt, divided

¼ teaspoon freshly ground black pepper, divided

2 tablespoons avocado oil

½ cup sliced yellow onion

1 garlic clove, minced

2 tablespoons sweet paprika

1 (15-ounce) can diced tomatoes, undrained

¼ cup low-sodium chicken broth

¼ cup sour cream

MACRONUTRIENTS: 60% Fat, 30% Protein, 10% Carbs

TO MAKE THE CHICKEN PAPRIKASH

1. Season the cut chicken thighs with ¼ teaspoon salt and ⅛ teaspoon pepper.

2. Heat the oil in a large skillet over medium heat until hot but not smoking. Add the chicken strips and cook, stirring often, for 3 to 4 minutes or until the chicken is about half cooked.

3. Add the onion and garlic and cook for an additional 4 to 5 minutes, until the onion starts to soften and is translucent.

4. Add the paprika to the skillet and cook for 1 minute. Be careful because paprika will burn. You want to heat it through to release the flavor.

5. Add the diced tomatoes and chicken broth and simmer for 5 to 6 minutes, until the sauce has thickened and reduced by about a third.

6. Season with the remaining salt and remaining pepper and turn off the heat. Whisk in the sour cream. Serve over mashed cauliflower.

7. Refrigerate any leftovers in an airtight container for 3 to 4 days.

FOR THE MASHED CAULIFLOWER

1 head cauliflower, trimmed, core removed and cut into large florets

2 tablespoons salted butter

2 or 3 tablespoons heavy cream

Kosher salt

Freshly ground black pepper

TO MAKE THE MASHED CAULIFLOWER

8. Place the cauliflower in a medium saucepan. Cover it with water and bring to a simmer over medium-high heat. Simmer for 10 to 12 minutes or until the cauliflower is very tender.

9. Drain the cauliflower well and pulse it in a food processor until it is very smooth.

10. Add the butter and cream and mix well. Season with salt and pepper to taste.

11. Store any leftovers in the fridge for 3 to 4 days.

SUBSTITUTION TIP: Mashed turnip is also tasty and low in net carbs. Prepare it like the cauliflower, but peel and dice the turnip first.

PER SERVING: Calories: 357; Total fat: 24g; Saturated fat: 9g; Protein: 26g; Total carbohydrates: 11g; Fiber: 5g; Erythritol: 0g; Net carbs: 6g Cholesterol: 140mg

Creamy Italian Chicken Skillet

PREP TIME: 10 minutes | **COOK TIME:** 15 minutes | **SERVES 4**

Inspired by the colors of the Italian flag—green, white, and red—this pretty dish scores high for being tasty and easy. It is almost a stir-fry. There's some up-front chopping, but once that's done, it is a breeze to prepare this dish.

1 pound boneless, skinless chicken breast, cut into ½-inch-thick slices

½ teaspoon kosher salt

¼ teaspoon freshly ground black pepper

2 tablespoons avocado oil

2 medium zucchini, halved lengthwise and cut into half-moons

1 red bell pepper, seeded and cut into strips

1 tablespoon Italian seasoning

1 garlic clove, minced

½ cup heavy cream

MACRONUTRIENTS: 57% Fat, 36% Protein, 7% Carbs

1. Season the chicken with the salt and pepper.

2. Heat the oil in a large skillet over medium heat. When the oil is hot but not smoking, add the chicken. Cook the chicken over medium heat, stirring often, for 5 to 6 minutes or until it is no longer pink inside.

3. Add the zucchini, bell pepper, Italian seasoning, and garlic and cook for 2 to 3 minutes or until the vegetables start to soften.

4. Add the cream and cook for 1 minute to combine all the flavors. Adjust the seasoning, if necessary, and serve.

5. Refrigerate any leftovers in an airtight container for up to 4 days.

SERVING TIP: Serve this hearty and colorful dish over zucchini noodles or your favorite shirataki noodles. Or enjoy it as it is. Kick up the heat a bit with a pinch of red pepper flakes, if you like it spicy.

PER SERVING: Calories: 315; Total fat: 20g; Saturated fat: 8g; Protein: 27g; Total carbohydrates: 6g; Fiber: 2g; Erythritol: 0g; Net carbs: 6g; Cholesterol: 105mg

Sweet-and-Sour Turkey

PREP TIME: 10 minutes | **COOK TIME:** 15 minutes | **SERVES 4**

With a delicious sweet-and-sour sauce coating tender and juicy cubes of turkey breast, this Asian-inspired dish is hard to beat. Pair it with your favorite cauliflower rice to scoop up all that yummy sauce.

1 pound boneless, skinless turkey breast, cut into 1-inch cubes

½ teaspoon kosher salt

¼ teaspoon freshly ground black pepper

1 tablespoon avocado oil

1 green bell pepper, seeded and cut into strips

½ cup sliced red onion

¼ cup water

2 tablespoons sugar-free ketchup

2 tablespoons brown sugar substitute

2 tablespoons apple cider vinegar

¼ teaspoon xanthan gum, to thicken, optional

MACRONUTRIENTS: 27% Fat, 67% Protein, 6% Carbs

1. Season the turkey with the salt and pepper.

2. Heat the oil in a large skillet over medium heat. When the oil is hot but not smoking, add the turkey cubes. Cook the turkey over medium heat, stirring often, for 5 to 6 minutes or until it is no longer pink inside.

3. Add the green bell pepper and onion and cook for an additional 2 to 3 minutes or until the vegetables start to soften.

4. Meanwhile, in a small bowl, whisk together the water, sugar-free ketchup, brown sugar substitute, and apple cider vinegar. Thicken with the xanthan gum, if using, by whisking it in.

5. When the turkey is cooked through, add the sauce to the skillet and heat it through, stirring often, about 3 minutes.

6. Serve with cauliflower rice or your favorite vegetables.

7. Refrigerate any leftovers in an airtight container for up to 4 days.

PER SERVING: Calories: 173; Total fat: 5g; Saturated fat: 1g; Protein: 27g; Total carbohydrates: 3g; Fiber: 1g; Erythritol: 6g; Net carbs: 2g; Cholesterol: 65mg

Coconut-Curry Chicken

PREP TIME: 5 minutes | **COOK TIME:** 15 minutes | **SERVES 4**

Rich, aromatic, and with a lovely color, this easy one-pot meal is ready in a jiffy. Use store-bought chicken stir-fry strips for even less prep time.

1 tablespoon avocado oil

½ cup sliced red onion

1 garlic clove, minced

1 tablespoon peeled and grated fresh ginger

1½ tablespoons yellow curry powder

1 (15-ounce) can full-fat coconut milk

¼ cup water

2 tablespoons sugar-free ketchup or tomato paste

1 pound boneless, skinless chicken breast, cut into strips

Kosher salt

Freshly ground black pepper

¼ cup chopped peanuts, for garnishing (optional)

½ jalapeño pepper, seeded and thinly sliced, for garnishing (optional)

Lime wedges, for garnishing (optional)

MACRONUTRIENTS: 62% Fat, 30% Protein, 8% Carbs

1. Heat the oil in a large skillet over medium heat. When the oil is hot but not smoking, add the onion. Cook the onion until it starts to soften, about 4 minutes.

2. Add the garlic and ginger and cook for 1 minute or until aromatic, then stir in the curry powder.

3. Meanwhile, in a medium bowl, whisk together the coconut milk, water, and ketchup. Add the mixture to the skillet, reduce the heat to low, and simmer for about 5 minutes, until the flavors have combined and the liquid has reduced a bit.

4. Add the chicken to the liquid and continue to cook over medium heat for 6 to 8 minutes, until the chicken is cooked.

5. Season to taste with salt and pepper and garnish with roasted peanuts, jalapeño, and fresh lime wedges (if using).

PER SERVING: Calories: 386; Total fat: 28g; Saturated fat: 20g; Protein: 28g; Total carbohydrates: 8g; Fiber: 2g; Erythritol: 0g; Net carbs: 6g; Cholesterol: 65mg

Mediterranean Chicken Bake

PREP TIME: 10 minutes | **COOK TIME:** 15 minutes | **SERVES 4**

Big, meaty chicken breasts are the star of this dish, but they can take forever to cook. When you butterfly them, cutting them open like a book, they cook much more quickly. Plus, there's more surface area for the tasty tomatoes, thyme, and feta that makes this dish such a hit.

1 pound boneless, skinless chicken breast, butterflied

1 teaspoon kosher salt, divided

½ teaspoon freshly ground pepper, divided

2 tablespoons avocado oil, divided

2 cups cherry tomatoes

2 cups sliced zucchini

1 teaspoon dried thyme, or 2 teaspoons fresh thyme leaves

1 cup crumbled feta cheese

MACRONUTRIENTS: 44% Fat, 48% Protein, 8% Carbs

PER SERVING: Calories: 277; Total fat: 14g; Saturated fat: 7g; Protein: 32g; Total carbohydrates: 6g; Fiber: 2g; Erythritol: 0g; Net carbs: 4g; Cholesterol: 98mg

1. Heat the oven to 375°F.

2. Season the chicken breasts with ½ teaspoon of salt and ¼ teaspoon of pepper.

3. Heat 1 tablespoon of the avocado oil in a large skillet over medium heat. When the oil is hot but not smoking, add the chicken breasts, working in batches if the skillet is too crowded.

4. Brown the chicken for 3 to 4 minutes, then flip it over and brown it on the other side.

5. Combine the tomatoes and zucchini in a medium bowl. Add the remaining 1 tablespoon of avocado oil, thyme, remaining ½ teaspoon of salt, and remaining ¼ teaspoon of pepper; toss well to coat.

6. Lay the chicken in a large casserole dish, and spread the tomatoes and zucchini around the chicken.

7. Cover with foil and bake for about 10 minutes or until the chicken reaches an internal temperature of 165°F. Remove the foil and sprinkle with the feta cheese.

8. Put the casserole under the broiler for 1 to 2 minutes to brown the cheese, then serve.

9. Refrigerate any leftovers in an airtight container for up to 4 days.

SAUSAGE AND RAPINI BAKE, PAGE 145

CHAPTER EIGHT

Meat

YOU CAN ENJOY A WIDE variety of meats while following a keto lifestyle, including hearty beef, pork, ham, and more. Avoid cooking boredom by trying something new. These tasty recipes have been designed with different flavor profiles in mind. From Asian-inspired dishes to comfort food classics, these hearty keto meat dishes are sure to please. Most of these recipes will pair well with a variety of sides. From plain cauliflower rice to a tasty side salad for extra greens, you can mix and match to make every meal different.

Beef Stroganoff Casserole

PREP TIME: 5 minutes | **COOK TIME:** 21 minutes | **SERVES 4**

This is a hearty and creamy dish. Mushrooms and beef pair nicely together, and a touch of sour cream adds to the richness of this family-favorite recipe. Using ground beef instead of chunks cuts down on the prep time, too.

2 tablespoons salted butter

1 pound mushrooms (white, cremini, or portobello), chopped

¼ cup sliced yellow onion

1 garlic clove, minced

1 pound 80% lean ground beef

4 ounces cream cheese

½ cup low-sodium beef broth

1 cup heavy cream

1 tablespoon Dijon mustard

½ teaspoon kosher salt

Freshly ground black pepper

Chopped fresh chives or parsley, for garnish

MACRONUTRIENTS: 75% Fat, 20% Protein, 5% Carbs

1. Melt the butter in a large skillet over medium heat. Add the mushrooms and onion and cook for 6 to 8 minutes, until the mushroom liquid has evaporated and the onion is soft.

2. Add the ground beef and brown it, breaking it up into chunks as it cooks.

3. When the beef is cooked and no longer pink, about 8 minutes, spoon out any residual fat, then add the cream cheese and stir it in until melted.

4. Add the beef broth and bring the mixture to a simmer. Simmer for 2 to 3 minutes to blend all the flavors.

5. Add the cream and Dijon mustard, and simmer for 1 to 2 minutes to slightly thicken.

6. Season the stew with the salt and pepper, garnish with chopped fresh herbs, and serve.

7. Refrigerate the leftovers in an airtight container for 3 to 4 days.

SUBSTITUTION TIP: Instead of beef, try this recipe with ground pork, chicken, or turkey.

PER SERVING: Calories: 584; Total fat: 49g; Saturated fat: 27g; Protein: 29g; Total carbohydrates: 8g; Fiber: 1g; Erythritol: 0g; Net carbs: 7g; Cholesterol: 202mg

Pork and Green Bean Stir-Fry

PREP TIME: 10 minutes | **COOK TIME:** 10 minutes | **SERVES 4**

Inspired by Chinese takeout dishes, this tasty stir-fry is a quick and easy recipe to pull together. Blanching the green beans first cuts down on the cooking time, and with plenty of vegetables, there's loads of fiber.

1 pound green beans, trimmed

1 tablespoon avocado oil

1 pound lean ground pork

¼ cup sliced red onion

1 clove garlic, minced

1 tablespoon peeled and grated fresh ginger

1 red bell pepper, seeded and cut into strips

¼ cup low-sodium chicken broth

3 tablespoons coconut aminos (or soy sauce)

1 teaspoon sesame oil

MACRONUTRIENTS: 66% Fat, 23% Protein, 11% Carbs

1. Bring a a large pot of salted water to a boil over high heat and add the beans. Boil for 1 minute, drain, and chill them in a large bowl of ice water. Drain the beans and set them aside.

2. Meanwhile, heat the oil in a large skillet over medium heat. Add the ground pork and cook for 3 to 4 minutes, breaking it up with a wooden spoon, until it is no longer pink.

3. Add the onion, garlic, and ginger and cook for an additional 2 minutes or until aromatic.

4. Stir in the bell pepper, blanched green beans, and chicken broth.

5. Increase the heat to medium-high heat and cook until the vegetables are heated through and the broth is mostly evaporated.

6. Add the coconut aminos and sesame oil. Mix well and serve.

7. Refrigerate the leftovers in an airtight container for 2 to 3 days.

> **SERVING TIP:** Garnish this colorful and tasty stir-fry with white or black sesame seeds and sliced scallions. Slice the scallions on an angle for a pretty presentation.

PER SERVING: Calories: 397; Total fat: 29g; Saturated fat: 10g; Protein: 23g; Total carbohydrates: 12g; Fiber: 4g; Erythritol: 0g; Net carbs: 8g; Cholesterol: 82mg

Salisbury Steak

PREP TIME: 10 minutes | **COOK TIME:** 15 minutes | **SERVES 4**

Salisbury steak is an American classic. Often found in diners and in frozen dinners, this version gets a boost of flavor while trimming the carbs. It's meaty, delicious, and easy to whip up on weeknights. Plus, the gravy is so good, you'll want to lick your plate clean.

1 pound 80% lean ground beef

¼ cup finely chopped yellow onion

1 large egg

4 teaspoons Dijon mustard, divided

1 teaspoon Worcestershire sauce

½ teaspoon garlic powder

1 teaspoon salt, divided

1 tablespoon avocado oil

1 cup low-sodium beef broth, divided

2 teaspoons tomato paste

¼ teaspoon freshly ground black pepper

¼ teaspoon xanthan gum, to thicken the gravy

MACRONUTRIENTS: 65% Fat, 32% Protein, 3% Carbs

1. In a medium bowl, mix the ground beef, onion, egg, 3 teaspoons of Dijon mustard, Worcestershire sauce, garlic powder, and ½ teaspoon salt. Combine the mixture well.

2. Form 4 patties from the ground beef mixture and set them aside.

3. Heat a large skillet over medium heat and add the oil, then the beef patties. Cook the patties for 4 to 5 minutes, flip them carefully, and cook for 5 to 6 minutes or until they're cooked through.

4. Remove the patties from the skillet and add ½ cup of beef broth. Scrape up all the bits from the bottom of the skillet, then add the remainder of the beef broth. Add the tomato paste and the remaining 1 teaspoon of Dijon mustard. Simmer the gravy for 3 to 4 minutes or until it has reduced by about one-quarter..

5. Season the gravy with the remaining salt and the pepper and thicken it with the xanthan gum.

6. Spoon the gravy over the Salisbury steak patties and dig in.

7. Refrigerate the leftovers in an airtight container for 3 to 4 days.

SERVING TIP: Serve this recipe with creamy mashed cauliflower or turnips to soak up all that amazing gravy.

PER SERVING: Calories: 304; Total fat: 22g; Saturated fat: 7g; Protein: 23g; Total carbohydrates: 2g; Fiber: 1g; Erythritol: 0g; Net carbs: 1g; Cholesterol: 124mg

Baked Bratwurst with Sauerkraut

PREP TIME: 5 minutes | **COOK TIME:** 30 minutes | **SERVES 4**

Bratwurst and sauerkraut go hand-in-hand in this Bavarian-inspired recipe. Look for big, meaty bratwurst for this dish, but read the labels to make sure there are no hidden starches. Use your favorite sauerkraut, and if it is too strong, don't be afraid to drain it and rinse it. Just make sure to squeeze out additional liquid before using it in this recipe.

16 ounces sauerkraut, drained

¼ cup thinly sliced yellow onion

1 tablespoon brown sugar substitute

1 teaspoon garlic powder

½ teaspoon kosher salt

¼ teaspoon freshly ground black pepper

1 pound bratwurst sausage links

MACRONUTRIENTS: 45% Fat, 39% Protein, 16% Carbs

1. Preheat the oven to 375°F.

2. In a medium bowl, mix the sauerkraut with the sliced onion, brown sugar substitute, garlic powder, salt, and pepper.

3. Arrange the sauerkraut mixture in the bottom of an 8-inch square casserole dish. Lay the bratwurst on top of the sauerkraut.

4. Cover and bake in the middle of the oven for 15 minutes, then take it out and stir the sauerkraut around. Put the baking dish back in the oven, uncovered, for 15 minutes or until the sausages are cooked to an internal temperature of 165°F.

5. Serve and enjoy.

6. Refrigerate the leftovers in an airtight container for 2 to 3 days.

SERVING TIP: Make sure to have a good German mustard on hand to serve with this dish.

PER SERVING: Calories: 196; Total fat: 10g; Saturated fat: 4g; Protein: 19g; Total carbohydrates: 8g; Fiber: 4g; Erythritol: 3g; Net carbs: 4g; Cholesterol: 34mg

Canned Corned Beef and Cabbage Skillet

PREP TIME: 10 minutes | **COOK TIME:** 20 minutes | **SERVES 4**

Canned corned beef can be found in most supermarkets. It is affordable and a great pick for a keto diet. It is, however, a bit higher in sodium, so be careful how much extra salt you add to this dish. Slice the cabbage very thinly so that it cooks quickly and evenly.

2 tablespoons salted butter

6 cups thinly sliced cabbage

¼ cup thinly sliced yellow onion

1 garlic clove, minced

1 (12-ounce) can corned beef

1 tablespoon apple cider vinegar

Kosher salt

Freshly ground black pepper

MACRONUTRIENTS: 64% Fat, 23% Protein, 13% Carbs

1. Heat a large skillet over medium heat and melt the butter. Add the cabbage and cook for 5 to 6 minutes, until the cabbage starts to soften.

2. Add the onion and garlic and cook for 5 to 6 minutes, until the cabbage is nearly tender.

3. Add the canned corned beef and break it up with a large spoon, keeping it in big, meaty chunks. Cook for 3 to 4 minutes or until the beef is heated through.

4. Season with salt and pepper to taste, and serve hot.

5. Refrigerate the leftovers in an airtight container for 3 to 4 days.

PER SERVING: Calories: 311; Total fat: 22g; Saturated fat: 9g; Protein: 18g; Total carbohydrates: 11g; Fiber: 3g; Erythritol: 0g; Net carbs: 8g; Cholesterol: 99mg

Southern Smothered Pork Chops

PREP TIME: 10 minutes | **COOK TIME:** 15 minutes | **SERVES 4**

Moist, tender, and juicy boneless pork chops are smothered in a rich onion and mushroom cream gravy in this recipe. Inspired by the flavors of the South, these chops are a comfort food classic. Pair this dish with green beans or broccoli for a pretty presentation.

2 tablespoons salted butter

1 to 1½ pounds boneless pork chops (about 4 chops)

½ teaspoon kosher salt

¼ teaspoon freshly ground black pepper

½ cup sliced yellow onion

8 ounces mushrooms, sliced

½ cup low-sodium chicken broth

4 ounces cream cheese

½ cup heavy cream

MACRONUTRIENTS: 68% Fat, 27% Protein, 5% Carbs

1. Heat a large skillet over medium heat and melt the butter. Season the pork chops with the salt and pepper, then add them to the hot skillet.

2. Cook the pork chops for 3 to 4 minutes per side, until browned. Remove the chops from the skillet and set them aside.

3. Add the onion and mushrooms to the skillet and cook them for 5 to 6 minutes, until the onion is soft and translucent.

4. Return the pork chops to the skillet and add the chicken broth. Bring to a simmer, then cook for 3 to 4 minutes or until the pork chops are no longer pink inside and reach an internal temperature of at least 145°F.

5. Turn off the heat and add the cream cheese, using a wooden spoon or spatula to melt it into the chicken broth.

6. Add the cream, adjust the seasoning, and serve.

7. Refrigerate the leftovers in an airtight container for 2 to 3 days.

PER SERVING: Calories: 449; Total fat: 35g; Saturated fat: 19g; Protein: 29g; Total carbohydrates: 5g; Fiber: 1g; Erythritol: 0g; Net carbs: 4g; Cholesterol: 163mg

Ground Beef and Cauliflower

PREP TIME: 5 minutes | **COOK TIME:** 15 minutes | **SERVES 4**

This Asian-inspired dish swaps in ground beef instead of other cuts so it cooks quickly. Frozen cauliflower also be used to cut down on the prep time. This dish tastes even better the next day, so don't worry about the leftovers. Serve it with cauliflower rice, or dig in to a bowlful of this meaty goodness all on its own.

1 tablespoon avocado oil

1 pound 80% lean ground beef

¼ cup sliced yellow onion

1 tablespoon peeled and minced fresh ginger

1 garlic clove, minced

¼ cup low-sodium beef broth

4 cups cauliflower florets (about 2 large crowns)

2 tablespoons coconut aminos (or soy sauce)

¼ teaspoon kosher salt

½ teaspoon sesame seeds, for garnishing

MACRONUTRIENTS: 67% Fat, 26% Protein, 7% Carbs

1. Heat the oil in a large skillet or wok over medium heat. Add the ground beef and cook, breaking it up with a wooden spoon or spatula, for about 4 minutes or until it is partially cooked.

2. Add the onion, ginger, and garlic, and cook for 2 to 3 minutes or until the beef is no longer pink. Spoon out any excess fat from the skillet and discard it.

3. Add the beef broth and cauliflower to the ground beef, increase the heat to medium-high, and cook for 2 to 3 minutes or until the cauliflower is tender.

4. Stir in the coconut aminos and salt. Adjust the seasonings if necessary, then top with the sesame seeds and serve.

5. Refrigerate the leftovers in an airtight container for 3 to 4 days.

PER SERVING: Calories: 361; Total fat: 27g; Saturated fat: 9g; Protein: 23g; Total carbohydrates: 8g; Fiber: 3g; Erythritol: 0g; Net carbs: 5g; Cholesterol: 81mg

Bacon Cheeseburger Skillet

PREP TIME: 5 minutes | **COOK TIME:** 20 minutes | **SERVES 4**

Bacon cheeseburgers go bunless in this tasty skillet recipe. Cleanup is a breeze because it is made in one pan. Don't forget the pickles—they add the right amount of tanginess to this meaty dish.

6 slices bacon, chopped into ⅓-inch-thick pieces

1 pound 80% lean ground beef

¼ cup diced yellow onion

1 garlic clove, minced

½ cup low-sodium beef broth

2 ounces cream cheese, at room temperature

2 tablespoons sugar-free ketchup

1 cup shredded sharp Cheddar cheese

½ cup diced dill pickles

MACRONUTRIENTS: 73% Fat, 25% Protein, 2% Carbs

1. Cook the bacon in a large skillet over medium heat until it is crisp. Remove the bacon from the skillet and reserve it on a plate.

2. Add the ground beef to the bacon fat in the skillet, still over medium heat, and use a spatula to break it up into chunks while cooking. Cook for about 4 minutes or until the beef is partially cooked.

3. Add the onion and garlic and continue to cook for 4 to 5 minutes, until the onion is soft and translucent.

4. Spoon out any excess fat from the skillet and discard it. Then, add the beef broth, bring the mixture to a simmer, and simmer for 5 minutes, uncovered.

5. Add the cream cheese and work it into the beef mixture until it is well combined. Add the sugar-free ketchup and mix it in. Turn off the heat.

6. Top the beef skillet with the cheese and the reserved bacon, and sprinkle the pickles over top. Dig in!

7. Refrigerate the leftovers in an airtight container for 4 to 5 days.

PER SERVING: Calories: 524; Total fat: 42g; Saturated fat: 18g; Protein: 32g; Total carbohydrates: 2g; Fiber: 0g; Erythritol: 0g; Net carbs: 2g; Cholesterol: 138mg

Sausage and Rapini Bake

PREP TIME: 10 minutes | **COOK TIME:** 25 minutes | **SERVES 4**

Inspired by hearty Italian casseroles, this tasty dish pairs meaty Italian sausage with rapini. Rapini, also known as broccoli rabe, is in the turnip family of vegetables and has a slightly bitter flavor that pairs well with sausage and creamy sauces. You'll find it in most large grocery stores, and it has small broccoli-like crowns with lots of leaves. You eat the whole plant—stems, leaves, and small florets. Just trim off the very bottom of the stems and discard any discolored leaves. Look for broccolini if you can't find broccoli rabe, but in a pinch, you can also use regular broccoli.

1 tablespoon avocado oil

1 pound Italian sausage, casings removed

¼ cup diced yellow onion

1 garlic clove, minced

¼ cup low-sodium chicken broth

1 bunch rapini (broccoli rabe), chopped

2 ounces cream cheese, at room temperature

¼ cup heavy cream

Kosher salt

Freshly ground black pepper

½ cup grated parmesan cheese

MACRONUTRIENTS: 80% Fat, 16% Protein, 4% Carbs

1. Preheat the oven to 350°F.

2. Heat the oil in a medium skillet over medium heat. Add the sausage, and use a wooden spoon or spatula to break it up into small chunks. Cook for 5 to 6 minutes or until the sausage is no longer pink.

3. Add the onion and cook for 3 to 4 minutes, until the onion starts to soften, then add the garlic and cook for 1 minute or until the garlic is aromatic.

4. Add the chicken broth and bring to a simmer. Add the rapini, cover the skillet, and simmer for 2 to 3 minutes or until the rapini is bright green and the leaves start to wilt.

5. Turn off the heat and mix in the cream cheese and cream. Season with salt and pepper to taste.

CONTINUES ⟶

6. Transfer the mixture to an 8-inch square casserole dish and top with the parmesan cheese. Cover with aluminum foil and bake for about 10 minutes or until the casserole is hot and bubbling. Remove the foil and turn on the broiler. Broil on high for 2 minutes or until the parmesan cheese starts to brown. Serve and enjoy.

7. Refrigerate the leftovers in an airtight container for 3 to 4 days.

PREP TIP: Removing the casings from the sausage can be messy, but not if you take a sharp paring knife and slit the casing from one end of the sausage to the other. Then, it's a simple matter of peeling off the casing and popping the sausage into the skillet.

PER SERVING: Calories: 593; Total fat: 53g; Saturated fat: 20g; Protein: 23g; Total carbohydrates: 6g; Fiber: 2g; Erythritol: 0g; Net carbs: 4g; Cholesterol: 133mg

Ham and Asparagus Casserole

PREP TIME: 10 minutes | **COOK TIME:** 20 minutes | **SERVES 4**

Ham and asparagus are perfect together, and in this tasty recipe, they are smothered in a delicious cheese sauce that'll have you licking your plate clean. It's an easy and impressive casserole that pairs nicely with a side salad for a hearty meal. Look for a large chunk of ham that you can dice; sliced deli ham won't work quite as well in this dish.

1 tablespoon avocado oil

¼ cup diced yellow onion

½ cup low-sodium chicken broth

4 ounces cream cheese

¼ cup heavy cream

1 pound ham, diced

1 pound asparagus, trimmed and cut into 1-inch pieces

1 cup shredded Swiss cheese

MACRONUTRIENTS: 62% Fat, 29% Protein, 9% Carbs

1. Preheat the oven to 350°F.

2. Heat the oil in a medium skillet over medium heat. Add the onion and cook for 4 to 5 minutes or until it is soft and translucent.

3. Add the chicken broth, cream cheese, and cream and bring to a simmer, breaking up the cream cheese until it is all mixed in. Turn off the heat.

4. Transfer the sauce to a large bowl and add the ham and asparagus, mixing well to coat everything.

5. Transfer the mixture to an 8-inch square casserole dish and top with Swiss cheese. Bake for 20 minutes or until the mixture is hot and bubbly. Enjoy.

6. Refrigerate the leftovers in an airtight container for 3 to 4 days.

SUBSTITUTION TIP: Swiss cheese has a strong and distinct flavor, but you can easily swap the Swiss for Jarlsberg. Jarlsberg has a milder flavor that works nicely in this recipe. Cheddar would also be fine.

PER SERVING: Calories: 429; Total fat: 30g; Saturated fat: 15g; Protein: 32g; Total carbohydrates: 10g; Fiber: 3g; Erythritol: 0g; Net carbs: 7g; Cholesterol: 123mg

MINI STRAWBERRY CHEESECAKES, PAGE 150

CHAPTER NINE

Desserts

ONE OF THE NICE THINGS about following a keto lifestyle is that, once you've eliminated carbs from your diet, your cravings for something sweet will also likely be reduced. Nevertheless, it's still nice to have a variety of easy, go-to recipes for when you want a little bit of something extra. I've designed these recipes for flavor—they're all lightly sweetened and packed full of wonderful tastes and textures. Some of them even keep well in the freezer, so you can nibble on them whenever you need a bite of something sweet.

Mini Strawberry Cheesecakes

PREP TIME: 10 minutes | **COOK TIME:** 18 minutes | **SERVES 6**

Subtly sweet, creamy, and easy to make, mini cheesecakes are the perfect choice whenever you need a bite of something decadent. This recipe makes six mini cheesecakes, and you can pop them in the freezer to enjoy later. Use muffin liners to keep the cheesecakes from sticking to the pan while they bake.

1 (8-ounce) block cream cheese, at room temperature

¼ cup granulated white sugar substitute

1 large egg

1 tablespoon sour cream

¼ teaspoon pure vanilla extract

½ cup sliced fresh strawberries

MACRONUTRIENTS: 83% Fat, 10% Protein, 7% Carbs

1. Preheat the oven to 350°F. Line 6 cups of a regular-size muffin tin with parchment paper muffin liners.

2. Put the cream cheese in a medium bowl and add the sugar substitute. Using a hand blender or electric mixer, beat the sugar and cream cheese on high until the mixture is light and fluffy, about 3 minutes.

3. Add the egg, sour cream, and vanilla, and continue mixing until everything is well combined.

4. Divide the mixture among the 6 muffin tins. Bake for about 15 minutes or until the cheesecakes are set in the middle.

5. Allow the cheesecakes to cool in the muffin pan before removing them. When cool, top each with a few strawberry slices and enjoy.

6. Refrigerate the leftovers in an airtight container for 2 to 3 days, or freeze them for up to 3 months.

SUBSTITUTION TIP: Blueberries and raspberries are also great keto options, so swap the strawberries with another kind of berry.

PER SERVING: Calories: 150; Total fat: 14g; Saturated fat: 8g; Protein: 3g; Total carbohydrates: 3g; Fiber: 0g; Erythritol: 12g; Net carbs: 3g; Cholesterol: 74mg

Chocolate Mug Cake

PREP TIME: 10 minutes | **COOK TIME:** 2 minutes | **SERVES 4**

Mug cakes are your answer to what to have for dessert. Made efficiently in a single mug, everything is mixed together and then cooked quickly in the microwave for a quick and easy sweet snack. Top this chocolatey mug cake with a dollop of sweetened whipped cream (make your own by whipping heavy whipping cream with powdered sugar substitute) or a spoonful of keto-friendly ice cream (page 154).

1 tablespoon salted butter

¼ cup superfine almond flour

1 large egg, beaten

2 tablespoons unsweetened cocoa powder

2 tablespoons sugar-free dark chocolate chips (Lily's is a great brand of keto-friendly chocolate)

2 tablespoons granulated white sugar substitute

½ teaspoon baking powder

MACRONUTRIENTS: 76% Fat, 15% Protein, 9% Carbs

1. Place the butter in a microwave-safe coffee mug, and heat on high for 20 seconds or until melted.

2. Add the almond flour, beaten egg, cocoa powder, chocolate chips, sugar substitute, and baking powder; mix well.

3. Cook the mug cake batter in the microwave on high for 45 seconds, and check to see if it is set. If it is still gooey, microwave it for an additional 15 to 20 seconds.

4. Let the cake cool for 2 to 3 minutes before enjoying.

5. Refrigerate any leftovers in an airtight container for up to 2 days.

SUBSTITUTION TIP: Swap the keto-friendly dark chocolate chips for white chocolate chips or caramel-flavored baking chips to change up the flavor of this mug cake.

PER SERVING: Calories: 84; Total fat: 7g; Saturated fat: 3g; Protein: 3g; Total carbohydrates: 3g; Fiber: 2g; Erythritol: 8g; Net carbs: 1g; Cholesterol: 54mg

Peanut Butter Cookie Dough Fat Bombs

PREP TIME: 10 minutes, plus 2 hours chilling time | **SERVES 4**

Perfectly snackable fat bombs keep in the fridge for weeks, so plan on keeping a few of these around for when you crave something sweet. Low in carbs and high in fat, fat bombs also help you bump up your macros if you're falling short for the day.

2 tablespoons salted butter, at room temperature

2 tablespoons cream cheese, at room temperature

2 tablespoons natural peanut butter

2 tablespoons granulated white sugar substitute

2 tablespoons superfine almond flour

¼ teaspoon pure vanilla extract

MACRONUTRIENTS: 85% Fat, 7% Protein, 8% Carbs

1. In a medium bowl, combine the butter, cream cheese, and peanut butter. Stir with a flexible spatula until the mixture is creamy and smooth.

2. Add the sugar substitute, almond flour, and vanilla extract and mix until combined.

3. Chill the cookie dough in the fridge for about 2 hours or until firm but not very hard. Then, scoop out about 2 tablespoons of the cookie dough and roll it into a ball. Repeat with the remaining dough.

4. Refrigerate the fat bombs in an airtight container for up to 1 week, or freeze them for up to 3 months.

PER SERVING: Calories: 142; Total fat: 14g; Saturated fat: 6g; Protein: 3g; Total carbohydrates: 3g; Fiber: 1g; Erythritol: 6g; Net carbs: 2g; Cholesterol: 23mg

Cheesecake Fluff with Raspberries and Almonds

PREP TIME: 10 minutes | **SERVES 4**

Raspberries and almonds add crunch and a pop of freshness to this simple recipe that's a lot like a rich, indulgent mousse. It's keto friendly, so indulge with this sweet treat. You can also use strawberries or blueberries instead.

⅔ cup heavy cream

6 ounces cream cheese, at room temperature

⅓ cup powdered sugar substitute

¼ teaspoon pure vanilla extract

½ cup raspberries

¼ cup slivered toasted almonds

MACRONUTRIENTS: 87% Fat, 6% Protein, 7% Carbs

1. In a medium bowl, whip the cream with a hand mixer on high speed until stiff peaks form, about 4 minutes. Set it aside.

2. In a second medium bowl, use the hand mixer, to whip the cream cheese, sugar substitute, and vanilla extract on high speed until light and fluffy, about 3 minutes.

3. Using a spatula, fold the whipped cream into the cream cheese mixture until well combined.

4. Divide the mixture among 4 pretty glasses or serving dishes, and top with the raspberries and almonds.

5. Cover any leftovers with plastic wrap, and store them in the refrigerator for up to 4 days.

COOKING TIP: Toasting almonds can be tricky. I like to toast them in a dry skillet on the stovetop over medium heat. That way, I can flip them around and pull them off the heat (and out of the skillet) as soon as they are golden brown.

PER SERVING: Calories: 325; Total fat: 32g; Saturated fat: 17g; Protein: 5g; Total carbohydrates: 6g; Fiber: 2g; Erythritol: 16g; Net carbs: 4g Cholesterol: 101mg

Easy No-Churn Keto Vanilla Ice Cream

PREP TIME: 10 minutes | **FREEZING TIME:** 6 hours | **SERVES 4**

Who doesn't love ice cream? With this keto version of no-churn ice cream, you can enjoy a cool and sweet treat any time. Top this vanilla ice cream with sugar-free syrup, fresh berries, or a sprinkle of sugar-free chocolate chips.

2 cups heavy cream

3 tablespoons powdered sugar substitute

½ teaspoon pure vanilla extract

MACRONUTRIENTS: 94% Fat, 3% Protein, 3% Carbs

1. In a medium bowl, use a hand mixer to whip the cream on high until it starts to thicken, about 3 minutes.

2. Add the sugar substitute and vanilla extract and whip for another 30 seconds to combine.

3. Transfer the whipped cream mixture to a deep freezer-safe container, like an ice cream container, and freeze for about 6 hours or overnight.

4. Use an ice cream scoop to scoop out a ½-cup serving of ice cream, and top it the way you like it.

5. Keep any leftovers in an airtight container in the freezer for up to a week.

PER SERVING: Calories: 412; Total fat: 44g; Saturated fat: 27g; Protein: 2g; Total carbohydrates: 3g; Fiber: 0g; Erythritol: 9g; Net carbs: 3g; Cholesterol: 163mg

Peanut Butter Mousse

PREP TIME: 10 minutes | **SERVES 4**

Rich, decadent, and lightly sweetened, peanut butter fans rave about this mousse. Plus, with only a handful of ingredients, it's also a quick and easy dessert to enjoy any time you've got a craving for something sweet.

4 ounces cream cheese, at room temperature

¼ cup natural peanut butter

1 cup heavy cream

3 tablespoons powdered sugar substitute

MACRONUTRIENTS: 87% Fat, 7% Protein, 6% Carbs

1. In a medium bowl, use a hand mixer or a spatula to blend the cream cheese and peanut butter until they're well mixed.

2. In a separate medium bowl, combine the heavy whipping cream and powdered sugar substitute. Use a hand mixer on high speed to whip the cream and sugar combination until stiff peaks form, about 4 minutes.

3. Using a spatula, fold the cream cheese and peanut butter mixture into the whipped cream until no streaks remain. Put the mousse into pretty serving dishes and serve.

4. Refrigerate any leftovers in an airtight container for 3 to 4 days.

SERVING TIP: Top your mousse with crushed roasted peanuts, a few sugar-free chocolate chips, or a dollop of whipped cream for an extra-decadent dessert.

PER SERVING: Calories: 399; Total fat: 40g; Saturated fat: 21g; Protein: 6g; Total carbohydrates: 6g; Fiber: 1g; Erythritol: 9g; Net carbs: 5g; Cholesterol: 133mg

GLUTEN-
FREE

NUT-
FREE

SOY-
FREE

VEGE-
TARIAN

Crème Brûlée

PREP TIME: 10 minutes, plus 4 hours chilling time | **COOK TIME:** 40 minutes
SERVES 4

With its signature crispy sugar topping and creamy, vanilla-scented interior, crème brûlée is sweet, decadent, and delicious. But it's also easy. There are a handful of ingredients in this recipe, and it turns out perfectly every time.

2 cups heavy cream
½ teaspoon pure vanilla
  extract
6 large egg yolks
½ cup granulated white
  sugar substitute

FOR THE TOPPING
¼ cup brown sugar
  substitute

MACRONUTRIENTS: 91% Fat,
6% Protein, 3% Carbs

1. Preheat the oven to 350°F.

2. Heat the cream in a medium saucepan over medium heat until it barely simmers. Turn the heat off and stir in the vanilla extract.

3. Meanwhile, in a medium bowl, whisk the egg yolks and the sugar with a hand mixer until the yolks are light in color and the sugar has dissolved, about 3 minutes.

4. Add ¼ cup of the hot cream to the egg mixture and mix on medium speed until it is well combined. Add half of the remaining cream and mix again, on medium speed, until combined. Add the remaining cream and mix on medium speed until combined.

5. Divide the mixture among 4 (8-ounce) ramekins. Set the ramekins in an oven-safe casserole dish that holds them without crowding. Fill the casserole dish with enough hot tap water so it comes halfway up the sides of the ramekins.

6. Transfer the casserole dish and the ramekins to the oven; bake for about 40 minutes or until they are set in the middle but still a bit jiggly.

7. Remove the casserole dish from the oven and let the custards cool on the counter for about 1 hour, then refrigerate them until cold, about 4 hours or overnight. Cover the ramekins with plastic wrap if you're going to chill them overnight.

8. When you're ready to serve them, sprinkle 1 tablespoon of brown sugar substitute over the top of each, and put the ramekins under the broiler to melt the sugar. You can also use a culinary torch to caramelize the sugar.

9. Cover any leftovers with plastic wrap, and refrigerate for 3 to 4 days.

PER SERVING: Calories: 494; Total fat: 51g; Saturated fat: 29g; Protein: 6g; Total carbohydrates: 4g; Fiber: 0g; Erythritol: 36g; Net carbs: 4g; Cholesterol: 440mg

Chocolate Nut Clusters

PREP TIME: 10 minutes, plus 1 hour chilling time | **MAKES 8** clusters

These bite-size treats are the perfect dessert. Sweet, crunchy, and covered in chocolate, they can be made with any combination of your favorite keto-friendly nuts and seeds. Pecans, almonds, a few peanuts, pepitas, sesame seeds, and more are all low in net carbs, making this a sinfully delicious dessert that's also keto friendly. Line a baking sheet with parchment paper for easy cleanup after the clusters have set.

¼ cup sugar-free dark chocolate chips (such as Lily's)

½ teaspoon coconut oil

¾ cup mixed nuts

MACRONUTRIENTS: 25% Fat, 5% Protein, 20% Carbs

1. Combine the dark chocolate chips and coconut oil in a medium microwave-safe bowl. Heat for 30 seconds on high, stir, and repeat until the chocolate chips are melted.

2. Add the nuts and mix until they're all coated.

3. Use a large spoon to scoop out a spoonful of the mixture and drop it onto a parchment paper–lined baking sheet. You should get 8 clusters.

4. Refrigerate the clusters for at least 1 hour to let them set. Store any leftovers in an airtight container at room temperature for up to a week.

PER SERVING (2 CLUSTERS): Calories: 205; Total fat: 17g; Saturated fat: 4g; Protein: 3g; Total carbohydrates: 10g; Fiber: 6g; Erythritol: 2g; Net carbs: 4g; Cholesterol: 0mg

MEASUREMENT CONVERSIONS

VOLUME EQUIVALENTS (LIQUID)

US STANDARD	US STANDARD (OUNCES)	METRIC (APPROX.)
2 tablespoons	1 fl. oz.	30 mL
¼ cup	2 fl. oz.	60 mL
½ cup	4 fl. oz.	120 mL
1 cup	8 fl. oz.	240 mL
1½ cups	12 fl. oz.	355 mL
2 cups or 1 pint	16 fl. oz.	475 mL
4 cups or 1 quart	32 fl. oz.	1 L
1 gallon	128 fl. oz.	4 L

VOLUME EQUIVALENTS (DRY)

US STANDARD	METRIC (APPROX.)
⅛ teaspoon	0.5 mL
¼ teaspoon	1 mL
½ teaspoon	2 mL
¾ teaspoon	4 mL
1 teaspoon	5 mL
1 tablespoon	15 mL
¼ cup	59 mL
⅓ cup	79 mL
½ cup	118 mL
⅔ cup	156 mL
¾ cup	177 mL
1 cup	235 mL
2 cups or 1 pint	475 mL
3 cups	700 mL
4 cups or 1 quart	1 L

OVEN TEMPERATURES

FAHRENHEIT (F)	CELSIUS (C) (APPROX.)
250°	120°
300°	150°
325°	165°
350°	180°
375°	190°
400°	200°
425°	220°
450°	230°

WEIGHT EQUIVALENTS

US STANDARD	METRIC (APPROX.)
½ ounce	15 g
1 ounce	30 g
2 ounces	60 g
4 ounces	115 g
8 ounces	225 g
12 ounces	340 g
16 ounces or 1 pound	455 g

REFERENCES

Arana, Maria Alonso, Jose Maria Valderas, and Josie Solomon. "Being Tested but Not Educated—A Qualitative Focus Group Study Exploring Patients' Perceptions of Diabetic Dietary Advice." *BMC Family Practice* 20, no. 1 (2019). doi.org /10.1186/s12875-018-0892-5.

Brownwell, Kelly D, and Jennifer L. Pomeranz. "The Trans-Fat Ban—Food Regulation and Long-Term Health." *The New England Journal of Medicine* 370, 19 (May 9, 2014): 1773–1775.

Centers for Disease Control and Prevention. "Diabetes: Diabetic Ketoacidosis." Accessed January 5, 2022. cdc.gov/diabetes/basics/diabetic-ketoacidosis.html.

Centers for Disease Control. "Diabetes: Heart Disease." Accessed January 5, 2022. cdc.gov/diabetes/library/features/diabetes-and-heart.html.

Cori, Carl F. and Gerty T. Cori. "The Carbohydrate Metabolism of Tumors: II. Changes in the Sugar, Lactic Acid, and CO2-Combining Power of Blood Passing Through a Tumor." *Journal of Biological Chemistry* 65, no. 2 (September 1925): 397–405. doi.org/10.1016/S0021-9258(18)84849-9.

Leonard, Jayne. "Foods That Are High in Electrolytes." May 15, 2020. medicalnewstoday.com/articles/electrolytes-food#foods.

Saslow, Laura R., Ashley E. Mason, Sarah Kim, Veronica Goldman, Robert Ploutz-Snyder, Hovig Bayandorian, Jennifer Daubenmier, Frederick M. Hecht, and Judith T. Moskowitz. "An Online Intervention Comparing a Very Low-Carbohydrate Ketogenic Diet and Lifestyle Recommendations Versus a Plate Method Diet in Overweight Individuals With Type 2 Diabetes: A Randomized Controlled Trial." *Journal of Medical Internet Research*, 19, no. 2 (February 2017): 27–42. doi:10.2196/jmir.5806.

Warburg, Otto, Franz Wind, and Erwin Negelein. "The Metabolism of Tumors in the Body." *Journal of General Physiology* 8, 6 (March 7, 1927): 519–530. doi:10.1085/jgp.8.6.519.

INDEX

ACKNOWLEDGMENTS

Jennifer Allen: I'd like to thank my husband, Matthew, for being so very supportive of all my projects. Also, to my son, Kegan: I'd never have become a successful blogger and recipe developer without you. Thank you for your ongoing encouragement. Brenna, your support is unparalleled. You're always optimistic and willing to jump in and help, and I'm the luckiest mom in the world to have you. Finally, a huge shoutout to my girls, Robin, Wendy, Brianne, Renee, and Kat: Thanks for being so awesome in so many ways.

Heather Ayala: Dr. Stephen Phinney, for being the one to provide me with my foundational education regarding the ketogenic diet through his YouTube videos and research articles. Joanna Foley, for putting her faith in my knowledge regarding the ketogenic diet and getting me connected to Callisto Media. And to the team at Callisto, for giving me an opportunity to participate in the writing of this book and guiding me along the way.

ABOUT THE AUTHORS

Jennifer Allen is a retired professional chef and author of several cookbooks, including *Keto Soup Cookbook*. Living in Texas for more than twenty years has inspired her recipe creation, with lively Southwestern flavors popping up in many of her recipes. She's now cooking north of the border in Ontario, Canada, where she lives with her family, four-legged best friend, and the cats who rule them all. She continues to post her recipes at ketocookingwins.com and also creates non-keto recipes which can be found at cookwhatyoulove.com.

Heather Ayala is a registered dietitian with a master of science in nutrition and is a Board Certified Ketogenic Nutrition Specialist. Heather has provided nutrition counseling to individuals struggling with a wide variety of acute and chronic health conditions, from diabetes to substance use disorder and everything in between. She loves people to no end and is absolutely passionate about seeing individuals and families thrive.

CPSIA information can be obtained
at www.ICGtesting.com
Printed in the USA
JSHW051420090922
30228JS00001B/2